The Creative Curriculum® *for* Preschool

Teaching Guide
featuring the Clothes Study

Kai-leé Berke, Carol Aghayan, Cate Heroman

TeachingStrategies® · Washington, D.C.

English editing: Lydia Paddock, Jayne Lytel, Diane Silver
Design and layout: Jeff Cross, Amy Jackson, Abner Nieves
Spanish translation: Claudia Caicedo Núñez
Spanish editing: Judith F. Wohlberg, Alicia Fontán
Cover design: Laura Monger Design

Teaching Strategies, Inc.
P.O. Box 42243
Washington, DC 20015

www.TeachingStrategies.com

978-1-60617-385-5

Library of Congress Cataloging-in-Publication Data

Berke, Kai-leé.
  The creative curriculum for preschool teaching guide featuring the clothes
study / Kai-leé Berke, Carol Aghayan, Cate Heroman.
       p. cm.
  ISBN 978-1-60617-385-5
  1. Education, Preschool--United States--Case studies. 2. Preschool
teaching--United States--Case studies. I. Aghayan, Carol. II. Heroman, Cate.
III. Title.
  LB1140.23.B473 2010
  372.139--dc22
                              2010002604

Teaching Strategies and *The Creative Curriculum* names and logos are registered trademarks of Teaching Strategies, Inc., Washington, D.C. This *Teaching Guide* is based on the *Clothes Study Starter* (Charlotte Stetson, lead author). Brand name products of other companies are given for illustrative purposes only and are not required for implementation of the curriculum.

1 2 3 4 5 6 7 8 9 10   17 16 15 14 13 12 11 10
     Printing   Year Printed

Printed and bound in United States of America

Acknowledgments

Many people helped with the creation of this *Teaching Guide* and the supporting teaching tools. We would like to thank Hilary Parrish Nelson for her guidance as our supportive Editorial Director and Jo Wilson for patiently keeping us on task. Both Hilary and Jan Greenberg provided a thoughtful and detailed content review that strengthened the final product.

Sherrie Rudick, Jan Greenberg, and Larry Bram deserve recognition for creating the first-ever children's book collection at Teaching Strategies, Inc. Working with Q2AMedia, they developed the concept for each book and saw the development process through from start to finish. Their hard work, creativity, patience, and attention to detail shines through in the finished product.

We are grateful to Dr. Lea McGee for her guidance, review, and feedback on our *Book Discussion Cards*. Jan Greenberg and Jessika Wellisch interpreted her research on a repeated read-aloud strategy to create a set of meaningful book discussion cards.

Thank you to Heather Baker, Toni Bickart, and Dr. Steve Sanders for writing more than 200 *Intentional Teaching Cards*, carefully aligning each teaching sequence with the related developmental progression and ensuring that children will receive the individualized instruction that they need to be successful learners. We are grateful to Sue Mistrett, who carefully reviewed each card and added strategies for including all children.

Translating *Mighty Minutes* into Spanish, ensuring cultural and linguistic appropriateness, was no easy task. Thank you to our dedicated team of writers and editors, including Spanish Educational Publishing, Dawn Terrill, Giuliana Rovedo, and Mary Conte.

Our brilliant editorial team, Toni Bickart, Lydia Paddock, Jayne Lytel, Diane Silver, Heather Schmitt, Heather Baker, Judy Wohlberg, Dawn Terrill, Giuliana Rovedo, Victory Productions, Elizabeth Tadlock, Reneé Fendrich, Kristyn Oldendorf, and Celine Tobal reviewed, refined, questioned, and sometimes rewrote our words, strengthening each page they touched.

Thank you to our Creative Services team for taking our words and putting them into a design that is both beautiful and easily accessible. The creative vision of Margot Ziperman, Abner Nieves, Jeff Cross, and Amy Jackson is deeply appreciated.

Our esteemed Latino Advisory Committee helped us continually reflect on how to support Spanish-speaking children and guided us through the development process. Thank you to Dr. Dina Castro, Dr. Linda Espinosa, Antonia Lopez, Dr. Lisa Lopez, and Dr. Patton Tabors.

We would like to acknowledge Lilian Katz and Sylvia Chard for their inspiring work on the Project Approach that has greatly advanced our thinking about quality curriculum for young children.

Most importantly, we would never be able to do this without the visionary guidance of Diane Trister Dodge. Her thoughtful leadership and commitment to young children and their families inspires all of the work that we do at Teaching Strategies.

Table of Contents

Getting Started

Why Investigate Clothes?

Children are interested in clothes from a very young age. Babies tug at their clothing; toddlers study buttons, snaps, and zippers; and, by the time children are in preschool, they develop distinct preferences for colors, fabrics, and styles. Children's interest in clothing can be the foundation for learning about different kinds of clothes, a variety of fabrics, the processes involved in making and selling clothes, the specialized purposes of some garments, and how clothes have changed over time.

This study shows how to use children's interest in clothes to help them explore social studies and science concepts about different kinds of clothing and where and how clothing is made. The study also helps children use skills in literacy, math, technology, and the arts as they investigate.

How do the children in your room show their interest in clothes? What do they say about clothes?

Web of Investigations

The *Teaching Guide featuring the Clothes Study* includes seven investigations aimed at exploring the world of clothes. The investigations offer children an opportunity to learn more about a particular aspect of clothing, such as special work uniforms or the manufacturing process.

Sometimes they include site visits and guest speakers. Each investigation strengthens a child's language and literacy skills, social and emotional growth, math comprehension, and physical development. Expand this web by adding your own ideas, particularly about clothing that is unique to your community.

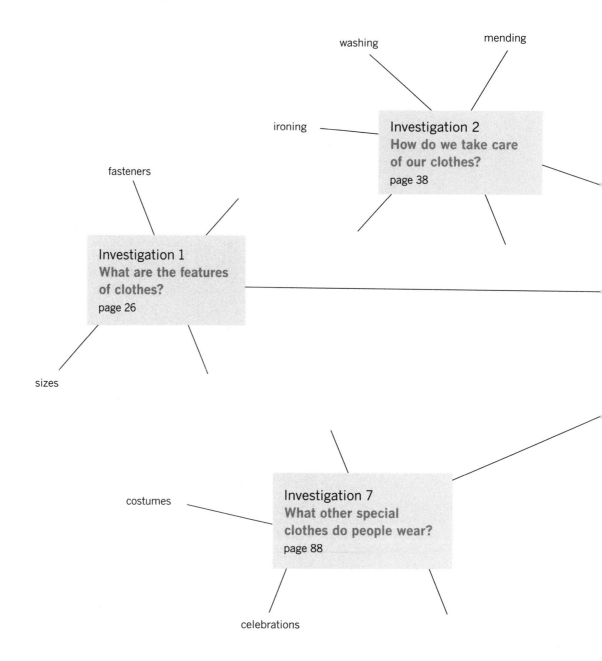

washing

mending

ironing

Investigation 2
How do we take care of our clothes?
page 38

fasteners

Investigation 1
What are the features of clothes?
page 26

sizes

costumes

Investigation 7
What other special clothes do people wear?
page 88

celebrations

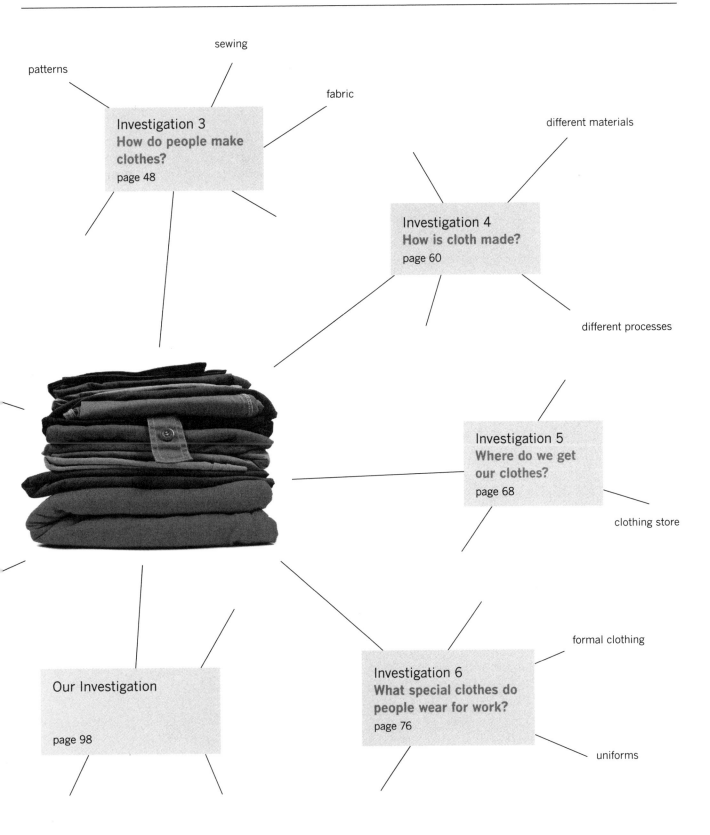

sewing

patterns

Investigation 3
How do people make clothes?
page 48

fabric

different materials

Investigation 4
How is cloth made?
page 60

different processes

Investigation 5
Where do we get our clothes?
page 68

clothing store

Our Investigation

page 98

Investigation 6
What special clothes do people wear for work?
page 76

formal clothing

uniforms

A Letter to Families

Send families a letter introducing the study. Use the letter to communicate with families and to invite their participation in the study.

Dear Families,

We recently noticed that the children are very interested in clothes. They talk about clothes, put them on and take them off, compare clothes, and add clothing details to their drawings. We think clothes will make an interesting study.

We need your help to gather a collection of clothes to investigate. We need clothes of all sizes, types, colors, and fabrics. Here's a list of suggestions, but you may also send in clothes that are not on the list. Please label the clothes with your name so we can return them to you at the end of our study. We promise to take good care of them!

jackets, coats, parkas, windbreakers, raincoats, ponchos, suit coats, blazers, vests, sweaters, sweatshirts, T-shirts, turtlenecks, work shirts, dress shirts, blouses,	flannel shirts, jeans, trousers, pants, skirts, dresses, shorts, pajamas, bathrobes, neckties, bow ties, bandanas, scarves, belts, sashes, suspenders, gloves, mittens, socks,	tights, shoes, boots, sandals, bathing suits, exercise clothes, old-fashioned clothes, uniforms, costumes, and more

As we study clothes, we will learn concepts and skills in literacy, math, science, social studies, the arts, and technology. We'll also use thinking skills to investigate, ask questions, solve problems, make predictions, and test our ideas.

What You Can Do at Home

Talk with your child about clothes. Examine the fabrics together and discuss how the clothes were made. Look at the labels to find out where the clothes were made and identify the fabric. Look at pictures from the past and note how the clothing differs from clothing today.

Teach your child to stitch. Use a large plastic needle and yarn; make stitches on burlap or felt.

When you shop for clothes, help your child notice how clothes are organized in the store and offer a simple explanation of how you compare prices.

At the end of our study, we'll have a special event to show you what we've learned. Thank you for playing an important role in our learning.

Carta a las familias

Envíele una carta a las familias para informarles sobre el estudio. Use la carta para comunicarse y como una oportunidad para invitarles a participar.

Apreciadas familias,

Nosotros hemos notado que los niños tienen gran interés en la ropa. Ellos hablan acerca de las prendas de vestir, se las ponen y se las quitan, las comparan y las añaden en sus dibujos como detalles. Por eso, creemos que un estudio de la ropa puede ser interesante.

Para realizar nuestro estudio, necesitamos de su ayuda para poder reunir una serie de prendas con el fin de investigarlas. Como necesitamos ropa de distintos tamaños, tipos, colores y telas, a continuación ofrecemos algunas sugerencias, pero siéntanse libres para enviar cualquier prenda de vestir que no esté incluida en la lista.

Por favor, escriban su nombre en sus prendas de vestir. Así podremos devolvérselas al final de nuestro estudio. ¡Les prometemos que las cuidaremos muy bien!

chaquetas, abrigos, parkas, chaquetas contra el viento, impermeables, ponchos, chaquetas de trajes, *blazers*, chalecos, suéteres, camisetas, camisetas de cuello alto, camisetas de trabajo,	camisas, camisas de franela, pantalones, *jeans*, faldas, vestidos, pantalones cortos, pijamas, salidas de baño, corbatas, corbatines, pañoletas, pañuelos, correas, guantes, mitones,	medias, medias-pantalón, zapatos, botas, sandalias, traje de baño, ropa para hacer ejercicio, ropa de otras épocas, uniformes, y muchos más

A medida que estudiemos la ropa, se aprenderán conceptos y se desarrollarán destrezas en lectoescritura, matemáticas, ciencias, estudios sociales, tecnología y las artes, al tiempo que se desarrolla el pensamiento investigando, haciendo preguntas, resolviendo problemas, haciendo predicciones y comprobando ideas.

Qué se puede hacer en el hogar

Hablen con los niños acerca de la ropa. Examinen juntos las telas y comenten cómo fue fabricada la ropa. Miren las etiquetas para saber dónde fue hecha e identifiquen las telas. Miren fotos de otras épocas y comenten cómo ha cambiado la ropa desde ese momento hasta nuestros días.

Enseñen a su niño o niña a coser. Usen agujas grandes de plástico e hilo grueso; hagan puntadas en arpillera o fieltro.

Cuando compren ropa, hagan notar a los niños cómo están organizadas las distintas prendas en el almacén y expliquen de manera sencilla cómo comparar los precios.

Al finalizar nuestro estudio, tendremos un evento especial para celebrar lo aprendido. De antemano, les agradecemos su participación y su importante rol en nuestro aprendizaje.

Beginning the Study

Introducing the Topic

To begin this study, you will explore the topic with the children to answer the following questions: What do we know about clothes? What do we want to find out about clothes?

Begin gathering many different types of clothes that you will use throughout the study. Ask the children, their families, and friends to help you build the collection. A sample letter to families is included in the beginning of this *Teaching Guide*. Below are some suggestions for different kinds of clothes to gather.

Programs must be vigilant about head lice, so hats were not included in the list below. Check your program guidelines for information on including hats in your classroom.

Build on children's natural interest in clothing as your clothing collection arrives in the classroom. Think about how to store and display the collection. Make the clothes available for children to wear and examine. You probably already have some clothes in your Dramatic Play area, but consider how to make room for more once the collection begins to grow. You might bring in a clothes rack and hangers, suspend a rod from the ceiling, or hang clothes on hooks or nails on walls.

Children are going to be very interested in this growing collection, so make sure they can see the clothes easily.

English-language learners
Write the words that name an article of clothing both in English and children's home languages on a card. Attach it to the clothing. That will help introduce words in a new language or languages to all of the children.

As clothes begin to accumulate, start talking about them. Have children describe the colors, style, and textures of the clothes. Teach new vocabulary for naming and describing the articles of clothing. Ask children to help you decide how to group the clothes as you display and label them.

jackets, coats	jeans, trousers, other long pants	gloves, mittens
parkas, windbreakers		socks, tights
raincoats, ponchos	skirts, dresses, kilts	shoes, boots, sandals
suit coats, blazers	shorts	bathing suits
sweaters, sweatshirts	pajamas, bathrobes	exercise clothes
T-shirts, turtlenecks	neckties, bow ties	old-fashioned clothes
work shirts, dress shirts, blouses, flannel shirts	bandanas, scarves	uniforms
	belts, sashes	costumes
	suspenders	

Preparing for Wow! Experiences

The "At a Glance" pages list these suggested Wow! Experiences, which require some advance planning.

Investigation 1:	Day 3: A visit from a dad or another male family member
	Day 4: A visit from a family member with a baby
Investigation 2:	Day 1: Visit a laundromat (If you cannot schedule a site visit but your school has a washer and dryer, try to arrange a time for the children to observe the machines.)
Investigation 3:	Day 3: A visit from someone who sews
Investigation 4:	Day 1: A visit from someone who knits or crochets
Investigation 5:	Day 2: A site visit to a clothing store (If you cannot schedule a site visit, invite a family member who works at a clothing store to share his or her experiences.)
Investigation 6:	Days 4 and 5: A visit from someone who wears a uniform or costumes for work, recreation, or both

Exploring the Topic

What do we know about clothes?
What do we want to find out?

	Day 1	Day 2	Day 3
Interest Areas	Dramatic Play: clothing collection	Library: books about clothes	Dramatic Play: hangers and clothespins
Question of the Day	Did you wear clothes for hot weather, warm weather, or cold weather last weekend?	What colors are you wearing today?	What clothes are you wearing today?
Large Group	Song: "Purple Pants" **Discussion and Shared Writing:** Introduction to the Clothing Collection **Materials:** Mighty Minutes 03, "Purple Pants"; clothing collection	Song: "Scat Singing" **Discussion and Shared Writing:** What makes our clothes special? **Materials:** Mighty Minutes 14, "Scat Singing"; a favorite article of clothing	**Movement:** Dancing With Scarves **Discussion and Shared Writing:** Describing Clothing **Materials:** Scarves or fabric streamers; clothing collection Prepare a chart called, "What do we know about clothes?"
Read-Aloud	*Caps for Sale* Book Discussion Card 01 (first read-aloud)	*Uncle Nacho's Hat*	*Caps for Sale* Book Discussion Card 01 (second read-aloud)
Small Group	Option 1: I Wear This When... Intentional Teaching Card LL01, "Shared Writing" **Option 2: Exploring the Clothing Collection** Intentional Teaching Card LL01, "Shared Writing"; clothing collection Display the charts and save the information you record for later charts.	Option 1: Clothing Sorting Game Intentional Teaching Card M03, "Seek & Find"; clothing collection; large basket **Option 2: Sorting & Classifying Clothes** Intentional Teaching Card M05, "Sorting & Classifying"; objects that define boundaries; clothing collection	Option 1: Going on a Clothes Hunt Intentional Teaching Card M06, "Tallying"; clipboards; paper; pencil or crayons **Option 2: Organizing the Clothes Collection** Intentional Teaching Card M02, "Counting & Comparing"; clothing collection; cardstock paper
Mighty Minutes™	Mighty Minutes 07, "Hippity, Hoppity, How Many?"	Mighty Minutes 47, "Step Up," using the previous day's small group chart(s)	Mighty Minutes 47, "Step Up," using one of the charts from day 1

Day 4	Day 5	Make Time For…
Art: collage materials, fabric scraps, glue, scissors	Dramatic Play: doll clothes	## Outdoor Experiences **Exploring Scarves** • Bring scarves outdoors for exploration. • Use descriptive language as children experiment with the scarves, e.g., "You chose a red- and yellow-striped scarf. How can you make it move?" • Teach children spatial concepts as they move their scarves, e.g., "Can you move your scarf [high, low, fast, slow, in front of you, behind you, inside the circle]?" • If scarves are unavailable, use streamers, ribbons, or any long pieces of fabric.
Do you have a favorite shirt? Why?	What do you want to know about clothes?	
Song: "Scat Singing" **Discussion and Shared Writing:** What do we know about clothes? **Materials:** Mighty Minutes 14, "Scat Singing"	Game: Just Like Mine **Discussion and Shared Writing:** What do we want to find out about clothes? **Materials:** Mighty Minutes 02, "Just Like Mine"	**Clothing Conversations** • Ask children what they notice about their clothes outdoors, e.g., "They keep me warm," "I can feel the wind through my shirt," or "When I get sweaty, I take off my jacket." • Record their comments on a notepad and add them to the chart, "What do we know about clothes?" created during large-group time.
Llama Llama Red Pajama	*Caps for Sale* Book Discussion Card 01 (third read-aloud)	**Physical Fun** • Intentional Teaching Card P11, "Jump the River"
Option 1: Favorite Clothes Intentional Teaching Card LL01, "Shared Writing" **Option 2: Bookmaking** Intentional Teaching Card LL02, "Desktop Publishing"; digital camera; computer; paper; printer; bookbinding supplies; each child's word bank; Mighty Minutes 03, "Purple Pants"	Option 1: Setting the Table Intentional Teaching Card M01, "Dinnertime"; dishes; napkins; utensils; cups; placemats **Option 2: Button Match** Intentional Teaching Card M04, "Number Cards"; set of numeral cards; buttons	## Family Partnerships • Invite a dad or other male family member and a family member with a baby to visit the classroom during Investigation 1. • Ask the dad to bring a couple of shirts with him (especially ones that he'd feel comfortable contributing to the classroom clothing collection) and, if possible, a picture of himself when he was a baby. • Ask the family member with the baby to bring one or more items of clothing the baby wore as a newborn.
Mighty Minutes 28, "Counting Calisthenics"	Mighty Minutes 04, "Riddle Dee Dee"	

Exploring the Topic

What do we know about clothes?
What do we want to find out?

Vocabulary

English: *clothes*

Spanish: *ropa*

See Book Discussion Card 01, *Caps for Sale* (*Se venden gorras*), for additional words.

Large Group

Opening Routine

- Sing a welcome song and talk about who's here.

> See *Beginning the Year* for more information and ideas on planning your opening routine. See Intentional Teaching Card SE02, "Look Who's Here!" for attendance chart ideas.

Song: "Purple Pants"

- See Mighty Minutes 03, "Purple Pants."

- After singing the song one time, adapt it using the colors of each child's clothing, e.g., "Jessica wore a blue shirt...."

> Using children's names in songs makes them feel valued and captures their attention.

Discussion and Shared Writing: Introduction to the Clothing Collection

- Talk about the clothing that families have provided for the collection.

- Invite children to show the class anything special that their families contributed.

- Explain, "This week we will study the collection of clothes and explore all of your ideas about clothes, including why we wear certain kinds of clothes. Let's look at the question of the day and see why you wore certain clothes last weekend." (The question of the day is located on the "At a Glance" chart.)

Before transitioning to interest areas, talk about the new choices in the Dramatic Play area (clothes to explore) and how children can use them.

Choice Time

As you interact with children in the interest areas, make time to

- Observe what children are saying as they explore clothes in the Dramatic Play area.

- Ask questions to help them wonder, e.g., "Who wore these boots?"

- Record interesting observations.

> **Always give children time to explore new materials before planning more formal investigations. Listen for what they already know.**

Read-Aloud

Read *Caps for Sale*.

- Use Book Discussion Card 01, *Caps for Sale*. Follow the guidance for the first read-aloud.

Small Group

- **Option 1: I Wear This When…**

- Review Intentional Teaching Card LL01, "Shared Writing."

- Introduce the experience: "Let's think about all the different kinds of clothes you wear. I'll write the words on a chart so we can remember."

- If they need help, ask, "What kinds of clothes do you wear when you come to school? Play at home? Go someplace special? Go to sleep?"

Option 2: Exploring the Clothing Collection

- Review Intentional Teaching Card LL01, "Shared Writing."

- Using the clothing collection, have each child select one article to put on.

- Describe the clothing, e.g., colors, patterns, sizes, textures, words, and labels.

- On chart paper, write a sentence with the child's name and description of the selected article of clothing, e.g., "Shantwan wore a purple hat."

- Sing the description to the tune of "The Farmer in the Dell," e.g., "Ashley wore a striped shirt. She wore a striped shirt. Picka-packa-licka-lack, she wore a striped shirt."

English-language learners
Show children examples of each type of pattern or texture being described, because the vocabulary for these concepts may be particularly difficult for English-language learners. If possible, also use the children's home languages to talk about the patterns and textures.

Mighty Minutes™

- Use Mighty Minutes 07, "Hippity, Hoppity, How Many?"

Large-Group Roundup

- Recall the day's events.

- Invite the children to wear an article of clothing to school tomorrow that they would like to talk about.

Exploring the Topic

What do we know about clothes?
What do we want to find out?

Vocabulary

English: *special, fanned*

Spanish: *especial, abanicar*

Large Group

Opening Routine

• Sing a welcome song and talk about who's here.

Song: "Scat Singing"

• Review Mighty Minutes 14, "Scat Singing."

Discussion and Shared Writing: What makes our clothes special?

• Wear a special article of clothing and tell the children: "I'm wearing my special shirt. It's my favorite because it's purple, it has words written on it, and my mom gave it to me."

• Review the question of the day.

• Lead a discussion about the children's clothes. Give each child a chance to talk about his or her own clothing and how it is special, that is, interesting or important in a particular way.

• Record their ideas.

> Talk informally about the letters and their sounds as you write them. "Pants starts with the /p/ sound. That's the letter *P*. Pajamas start with a /p/ sound, too. Watch how I write a *P*."

Before transitioning to interest areas, talk about the new books about clothes in the Library area and any special clothes that have been added to the clothing collection in the Dramatic Play area.

Choice Time

As you interact with children in the interest areas, make time to

• Talk with children about their clothing during choice time.

• Record some of their words and stories about their clothing or any of the clothing in the collection.

• Read books about clothing in the Library area with children. Pay attention to what they find interesting.

> By spending time in the Library area, you encourage children's involvement in this important interest area.

Read-Aloud

Read *Uncle Nacho's Hat.*

- **Before you read**, talk about the title of the book. Say, "I wonder what this story is about."

- **As you read**, demonstrate the meaning of the word *fanned* by using your hand, a piece of paper, or a hat. After Uncle Nacho gets his new hat, ask, "What do you think he will do with his old hat?"

- **After you read**, help children recall their predictions about what they thought would happen to the hat. Compare them to what happened in the story.

English-language learners
Combining gestures with words helps children learn and use new vocabulary. This supports the language development of all children.

Small Group

Option 1: Clothing Sorting Game

- Review Intentional Teaching Card M03, "Seek & Find."

- Use the collection of clothes to play the game, saying, "I'm thinking of something you wear when… [it's raining outside, you go to bed, you go to a birthday party, etc.]."

- Have each child select an article of clothing that fits the category.

- Describe the chosen clothes and the category they belong to. For example, say, "A raincoat, a big hat, and rubber boots are all things that people might wear when it is raining."

- Put those items in a pile and continue with another category.

Option 2: Sorting & Classifying Clothes

- Review Intentional Teaching Card M05, "Sorting & Classifying."

- Ask the children, "How are some of our clothes alike? How are they different?"

- Help children sort each other by their clothes into categories of their choice, e.g., children wearing pants in one group and children in shorts in another.

If available, arrange hula hoops on the floor for children to use for sorting. Using hula hoops helps children see the groupings by providing clear boundaries around each group.

Mighty Minutes™

- Use Mighty Minutes 47, "Step Up."

- Use the chart(s) created in yesterday's small-group time.

- Invite children to step up and circle a word.

You are checking the child's understanding of a word as a unit of print, not whether the child can read the circled word.

Large-Group Roundup

- Recall the day's events.

- Invite children who looked at books about clothes during choice time to share what they learned or enjoyed about the books.

What do we know about clothes?
What do we want to find out?

Vocabulary

English: *tally, clothespins, coat hangers*

Spanish: *llevar la cuenta, pinzas para colgar la ropa, colgadores*

See Book Discussion Card 01, *Caps for Sale (Se venden gorras),* for additional words.

Large Group

Opening Routine

- Sing a welcome song and talk about who's here.

Movement: Dancing With Scarves

- Dance to music with fabric streamers or scarves.

Discussion and Shared Writing: Describing Clothing

- From the collection of clothes, let each child select an article of clothing and pass it around for others to examine.

- Ask questions, such as

   "Who might wear this?"

   "When might they wear it?"

   "What do you notice about this piece of clothing?"

   "Tell us about how this feels."

   "What size is this?"

   "What do you notice about the materials that this is made from?"

   "What do you think the person who wore these clothes did while wearing them?"

- Create a chart, "What do we know about clothes?" Record some of the children's ideas and words. You may also want to add the information you collected from small-group time on days 1 and 2.

> Pause after you ask a question. Some children may need more time to process your question before they are ready to respond. Invite children who usually respond quickly to think quietly for a moment, too. "Let's all think quietly about who might wear this. Hmmm... I'm thinking...."

Before transitioning to interest areas, talk about and show the clothespins and coat hangers for displaying the clothing collection. Ask, "What can we do with these things? What do you think they are called?" Describe the items and show, or let the children show, how to use them.

Ask the children for their help during choice time in hanging the clothing collection so that others can find particular clothes easily.

Choice Time

As you interact with children in the interest areas, make time to

- Listen to what the children are saying while they hang the clothes.

- Rephrase their words and expand their language. After a child says, "I hang up clothes at home," you might say, "You hang your clothes up at home. Where do you put them when you hang them up?"

> The simple task of hanging clothes develops strength and coordination in children's hands. This will be important as they learn to write.

Read-Aloud

Read *Caps for Sale*.

- Use Book Discussion Card 01, *Caps for Sale*. Follow the guidance for the second read-aloud.

Small Group

Option 1: Going on a Clothes Hunt

- Review Intentional Teaching Card M06, "Tallying."

- Tell the children that today they will go on a clothes hunt to count the number of people who are wearing certain types of clothes.

- Review the question of the day.

- Encourage them to think of categories for the types of clothes that they would like to count, e.g., the number of people wearing shorts, skirts or dresses, jackets, and hats.

- Have them use tally marks to help them count the items.

Option 2: Organizing the Clothes Collection

- Review Intentional Teaching Card M02, "Counting & Comparing."

- Gather children around the clothing collection. Ask, "What are some different kinds of clothes?"

- Review the question of the day.

- Categories children might suggest include baby clothes, outside clothes, dresses, and pants.

- Follow the guidance on the card using the children's suggested categories and the clothing collection.

Mighty Minutes™

- Use Mighty Minutes 47, "Step Up."

- Use one of the charts you created on day 1 of the investigation, and ask children to circle a letter.

Large-Group Roundup

- Recall the day's events.

- Ask children to share what they discovered during small-group time.

What do we know about clothes?
What do we want to find out?

Vocabulary

English: *fabric, pajamas, whimper, fret, weeping, wailing*

Spanish: *tela, pijamas, lloriquear, inquietarse, sollozar, lamentarse*

Large Group

Opening Routine

- Sing a welcome song and talk about who's here.

Song: "Scat Singing"

- Review Mighty Minutes 14, "Scat Singing."

Discussion and Shared Writing: What do we know about clothes?

- Tell the children that you are going to continue to record everything they already know about clothes.

- Record the children's ideas on the chart, "What do we know about clothes?"

- If necessary, use real clothes as prompts to stimulate ideas about what they know.

- Begin by recalling some of what children said earlier in the week, e.g., "Juan said some sweaters feel scratchy. Jenna said her mom makes her clothes with a sewing machine."

> This is a great time to give each child a small whiteboard or clipboard and paper so they can record their ideas by writing and drawing. This helps them focus on the discussion.

> Keep the chart, "What do we know about clothes?" available throughout the study so that you can add to it as children make new discoveries.

Before transitioning to interest areas, talk about the fabric scraps in the Art area for making collages.

Choice Time

As you interact with children in the interest areas, make time to

- Talk to children as they work on their collages.

- Describe the fabrics they choose.

- Ask open-ended questions to encourage thinking and discussion.

English-language learners
For English-language learners and other children with limited receptive and expressive skills in English, include questions that can be answered by either pointing to a piece of clothing or a picture, or by giving a one-word answer. For example, ask, "Which do you like best?" or "Which is the same color as your sweater?"

Read-Aloud

Read *Llama Llama Red Pajama*.

- **Before you read**, read the title of the book and encourage children to look at the cover. Ask, "What are *pajamas*? What do you think this story will be about?"

- **As you read**, use your voice to show the little llama's growing anxiety. Explain that the word, *fret*, means to worry. As you say the words *whimper, weeping,* and *wailing,* inflect your voice to help children understand their meaning.

- **After you read**, ask, "How did baby llama feel when his mother didn't come right away?" Invite the children to recall times when they've felt nervous at nighttime and who helps them feel safe.

When they are calm, talk to children about how to handle strong feelings. This helps them think about appropriate strategies for expressing strong emotions when they experience them in the future.

Small Group

Option 1: Favorite Clothes

- Review Intentional Teaching Card LL01, "Shared Writing."

- Ask children to describe their favorite clothes. Remind children of the question of the day.

- Record the color words they describe using a marker of the same color.

Option 2: Bookmaking

- Review Intentional Teaching Card LL02, "Desktop Publishing."

- Take digital photos of the children.

- Remind children of the question of the day.

- Use the photos of the children to make a book following the patter of Mighty Minutes 03, "Purple Pants."

Mighty Minutes™

- Use Mighty Minutes 28, "Counting Calisthenics."

Large-Group Roundup

- Recall the day's events.

- Share the book or shared writings that the children made during small-group time.

Day 5   Exploring the Topic

What do we know about clothes? What do we want to find out?

Vocabulary

See Book Discussion Card 01,
Caps for Sale (Se venden gorras), for words.

Large Group

Opening Routine

- Sing a welcome song and talk about who's here.

Game: Just Like Mine

- Use Mighty Minutes 02, "Just Like Mine."

> After you play a game that gets children active and moving around, make sure to end the game by calling them back together, e.g., "Find your spot on the rug and sit on it."

Discussion and Shared Writing: What do we want to find out about clothes?

- Post the chart, "What do we know about clothes?" near the large-group area so it can be referred to often.

- Say, "We know a lot of things already about clothes, but now let's think about what we want to find out about clothes."

- Model the questioning process for children, e.g., show the children a hole in clothes and wonder aloud how it could be fixed; talk about your clothes' being too tight or loose and wonder whether you bought the right size; talk about a puppet or baby doll that needs clothes and ask children whether they think the class could make some clothes for it.

- Write the questions on a new chart for the children to see. Call it, "What do we want to find out about clothes?" Help children formulate questions, e.g., if a child says, "I think we should make clothes," you can respond, "You think we should make clothes. We'll need to know how to make them. I'll write, 'How are clothes made?' and 'Can we make clothes?'"

- Refer to the question of the day and add the children's question(s) to the chart.

> As children pose questions throughout the study, add them to the chart. Helping children think about all the ways they can learn or find out about something is a very important life skill to include in every study.

Before transitioning to interest areas, talk about the doll clothes in the Dramatic Play area and how children may use them.

Choice Time

As you interact with children in the interest areas, make time to

- Listen carefully to children's discussions and observations as they play with the doll clothes.

- Describe their process of dressing and undressing the dolls. "You put her arm through the arm hole. You pulled the dress over her head."

Read-Aloud

Read *Caps for Sale*.

- Use Book Discussion Card 01, *Caps for Sale*. Follow the guidance on the card for the third read-aloud.

Small Group

Option 1: Setting the Table

- Review Intentional Teaching Card M01, "Dinnertime."

- Follow the guidance on the card.

Option 2: Button Match

- Review Intentional Teaching Card M04, "Number Cards."

- Follow the guidance on the card using buttons as the small manipulative.

Mighty Minutes™

- Use Mighty Minutes 04, "Riddle Dee Dee."

Large-Group Roundup

- Recall the day's events.

- Review the chart, "What do we want to find out about clothes?" with the children.

Investigating the Topic

Introduction

You have already started lists of children's ideas and questions about clothes. As you implement the study, you will design investigations that help them expand their ideas, find answers to their questions, and learn important skills and concepts. This section has daily plans for investigating the questions that children ask. Do not be limited by these suggestions. Use them as inspiration to design experiences tailored to your own group of children and the resources in your school and community. While it is important to respond to children's ideas and follow their lead as their thinking evolves, it is also important for you to organize the study and plan for possibilities. Review the "At a Glance" pages for suggested Wow! Experiences. These events require some advance planning.

Investigation 1

What are the features of clothes?

	Day 1	Day 2	Day 3
Interest Areas	**Art:** clothing of different sizes and features **Computer:** eBook version of *Goldilocks and the Three Bears*	**Blocks:** standard measuring tools, e.g., rulers, yardsticks, measuring tapes **Computer:** eBook version of *Goldilocks and the Three Bears*	**Library:** props from *Goldilocks and the Three Bears*
Question of the Day	What do you know about the story *Goldilocks and the Three Bears?*	Is the tag inside your shirt marked with a number or the letter *S, M,* or *L*? (Have sticky notes available for answers.)	What shapes do you see on your clothes?
Large Group	**Song:** "Farmer in the Dell" **Discussion and Shared Writing:** Exploring Sizes of Clothes **Materials:** Mighty Minutes 08, "Clap the Missing Word"; small article of clothing; small, medium, and large T-shirts; digital camera	**Rhyme:** "Riddle Dee Dee" **Discussion and Shared Writing:** Measurement Tools **Materials:** Mighty Minutes 04, "Riddle Dee Dee"; bag or box with a variety of standard measurement tools	**Game:** Finding Shapes on Clothing **Discussion and Shared Writing:** Looking at Large Clothes **Materials:** Mighty Minutes 20, "I Can Make a Circle"; shape cards; standard and nonstandard measuring tools; digital camera
Read-Aloud	*Goldilocks and the Three Bears*	*Goldilocks and the Three Bears* **Materials:** props to act out *Goldilocks and the Three Bears;* Intentional Teaching Card LL06, "Dramatic Story Retelling"	*A Pocket for Corduroy*
Small Group	**Option 1: Play Dough** Intentional Teaching Card M15, "Play Dough" (See card for equipment, ingredients, and recipe.) **Option 2: Biscuits** Intentional Teaching Card M10, "Biscuits" (See card for equipment, ingredients, and recipe.)	**Option 1: What's Missing?** Intentional Teaching Card LL18, "What's Missing?"; clothing collection; large piece of paper **Option 2: Memory Card Game** Intentional Teaching Card LL08, "Memory Games"; a memory game or set of duplicate pictures of clothing	**Option 1: Bigger Than, Smaller Than, Equal To** Intentional Teaching Card M09, "Bigger Than, Smaller Than, Equal To"; building blocks; measuring tools **Option 2: Measure & Compare** Intentional Teaching Card M12, "Measure & Compare"; clothing collection; nonstandard measuring tools
Mighty Minutes™	Mighty Minutes 18, "I'm Thinking Of …"	Mighty Minutes 20, "I Can Make a Circle"	Mighty Minutes 27, "Diddle, Diddle, Dumpling"

Day 4	Day 5	Make Time For...
Toys and Games: baby, child, and adult clothes; standard and nonstandard measuring tools **Computer:** eBook version of *Button, Button, Who's Got the Button?*	**Art:** materials to make thank-you notes	## Outdoor Experiences **Measuring Tools** • After introducing measuring tapes and rulers during large-group time, bring them outside for the children to use. • Provide clipboards and pencils for the children to record measurements of objects.
What size clothes do you think babies wear?	How many buttons do you have on your clothes?	**Physical Fun** • Intentional Teaching Card P12, "Exploring Pathways"
Rhyme: "Riddle Dee Dee" **Discussion and Shared Writing:** Baby Visit **Materials:** Mighty Minutes 04, "Riddle Dee Dee"; a few samples of baby clothes; digital camera	**Music:** Drums **Discussion and Shared Writing:** How do clothes stay on our bodies? **Materials:** drums; other objects that can be used as drums; shirt and pants with buttons	## Family Partnerships • Ask family members to bring in old baby clothes that their children wore as babies. • Invite families to access the eBooks, *Goldilocks and the Three Bears* and *Button, Button, Who's Got the Button?*
Button, Button, Who's Got the Button?	*The Mitten* Book Discussion Card 02 (first read-aloud)	## Wow! Experiences • Day 3: A visit from a dad or other male family member • Day 4: A visit from a family member with a baby
Option 1: Small, Medium, and Large Book Intentional Teaching Card LL04, "Bookmaking"; paper; pencils or crayons; binding materials **Option 2: Small, Medium, and Large Computer Book** Intentional Teaching Card LL02, "Desktop Publishing"; digital camera; computer; printer; bookbinding supplies; paper; each child's word bank	**Option 1: Tallying Features of Clothing** Intentional Teaching Card M06, "Tallying"; paper, clipboards, and pencils **Option 2: How Clothes Stay on Our Bodies** Intentional Teaching Card M11, "Graphing"; clothing fasteners, e.g., zippers, Velcro®, buttons, laces	
Mighty Minutes 74, "Jack in the Box"	Mighty Minutes 25, "Freeze"; dance music; letter cards	

Day 1 | Investigation 1

What are the features of clothes?

Vocabulary

English: *small, medium, large, size*

Spanish: *pequeño, mediano, grande, tamaño*

Large Group

Opening Routine

- Sing a welcome song and talk about who's here.

Song: "The Farmer in the Dell"

- Review Mighty Minutes Card 08, "Clap the Missing Word."

- Follow the guidance on the card using the song, "The Farmer in the Dell."

> In this activity, you are helping children sharpen their phonological awareness skills by listening for a particular word in a sentence.

Discussion and Shared Writing: Exploring Sizes of Clothes

- Pretend to struggle to put on a piece of a child's clothing that is obviously too small.

- Refer to the chart, "What do we know about clothes?" and say, "[Ashley] said clothes come in different sizes. So this must be the wrong size."

- Ask, "How can we find out what size clothes or shoes we wear?"

- Record their answers on a chart.

- Allow children to examine the label size in their own or each other's shirts or shoes and share or chart their responses.

- Lay out a small, medium, and large T-shirt and ask children what they notice about the shirts.

- Invite a couple of children to try on the shirts and talk about how they fit. Take photos of this experience.

Before transitioning to interest areas, talk to the children about how they can use their clothing display in the Art area to inspire paintings at the easels.

Choice Time

As you interact with children in the interest areas, make time to

- Observe how children use the clothing to inspire their paintings. Before they begin to paint, ask them a couple of

questions to spark their imaginations. "What do you notice about these clothes? Which one do you think is the most interesting? Why?"

Read-Aloud	Read *Goldilocks and the Three Bears*.	Tell the children that the book will be available to them on the computer in the Computer area.

Read-Aloud

Read *Goldilocks and the Three Bears*.

- **Before you read**, remind children about the question of the day. Ask, "What do you know already about the story?"

- **As you read**, talk about the sizes of the bears, bowls, chairs, and beds and relate this information to the sizes of the shirts discussed at group time.

- **After you read**, ask what props are needed to act out the story. List them on chart paper or a whiteboard. Invite the children to help you gather them.

Tell the children that the book will be available to them on the computer in the Computer area.

English-language learners
To help English-language learners identify props, have them point to objects in the book's illustrations or to objects in the room, such as chairs. Then confirm their comprehension and model language for talking about the items. For example, say, "Yes, we need a small chair to act out the story." Emphasize the name of the prop.

Small Group

Option 1: Play Dough

- Review Intentional Teaching Card M15, "Play Dough."

- After the play dough is made, invite children to create small, medium, and large objects.

Option 2: Biscuits

- Use Intentional Teaching Card M10, "Biscuits," to make biscuit dough with the children.

- Use small-, medium-, and large-sized biscuit cutters to cut out shapes or use the rims of glasses or cups to cut the biscuits. Talk to the children about the sizes as they work.

Mighty Minutes™

- Use Mighty Minutes 18, "I'm Thinking Of...."

Large-Group Roundup

- Recall the day's events.

- Invite children who painted at the easel during choice time to share their work inspired by the clothing display.

Day 2   Investigation 1

What are the features of clothes?

Vocabulary

English: *tape measure, yardstick, ruler, measure, long, short*

Spanish: *cinta para medir, vara para medir, regla, medir, largo, corto*

Large Group

Opening Routine

- Sing a welcome song and talk about who's here.

Rhyme: "Riddle Dee Dee"

- Review Mighty Minutes 04, "Riddle Dee Dee." Try the jumping syllables variation on the back of the card.

> **Using "Riddle Dee Dee" in this new way gives children practice with breaking words into separate syllables in a playful way.**

Discussion and Shared Writing: Measuring Tools

- Show pictures from yesterday's experience or remind children of the importance of choosing clothes that fit.

- Refer to the question of the day and sort sticky notes by size.

- Use a mystery bag or box to introduce or review a variety of standard measuring tools, e.g., tape measure, ruler, yardstick, foot measurer.

- Ask open-ended questions about the items, e.g., "What could I measure with this?" "Which one of these would be better for measuring how tall the door is?"

- Pass items around for children to examine.

- Demonstrate how to measure a person using a tape measure and talk about the importance of finding out the length of pants or a dress.

- Emphasize that our clothes and shoes come in different sizes so we have to measure our bodies to find our size.

> **Using a strategy such as a mystery bag helps children focus their attention. Being able to attend to a task is an important part of cognitive self-regulation.**

Before transitioning to interest areas, talk about the measuring tools in the Block area and how children can use them.

Choice Time	As you interact with children in the interest areas, make time to • Observe how they measure objects. • Encourage them to read the numerals on the tools.	• Provide paper and pencils for recording observations if the children are interested.
Read-Aloud	• Reread *Goldilocks and The Three Bears*. Invite the children to act out the story with the props gathered yesterday. • Refer to Intentional Teaching Card LL06, "Dramatic Story Retelling" for more information.	**Retelling stories helps children build comprehension skills. Read more about retelling in the section on teaching strategies in *The Creative Curriculum for Preschool, Volume 3: Literacy*.**
Small Group	**Option 1: What's Missing?** • Review Intentional Teaching Card LL18, "What's Missing?" • Follow the guidance on the card using clothing items to play the game. **Option 2: Memory Card Game** • Review Intentional Teaching Card LL08, "Memory Games." Follow the guidance on the card.	• Use any memory or lotto game that you have in your classroom or create one by gluing pictures of matching clothing items onto index cards. **These games help children improve their visual memory skills. This skill will be important in literacy development as children remember a letter or word. In math, they will use the skill to recognize numerals, shapes, and patterns.**
Mighty Minutes™	• Use Mighty Minutes 20, "I Can Make a Circle."	
Large-Group Roundup	• Recall the day's events. • Remind the children that a dad or other male family member is coming to visit the classroom tomorrow. Talk about the clothing size he might wear. Ask the children to think about questions to ask him about his clothing size and record their questions on the chart, "What do we want to find out about clothes?"	

Investigation 1

What are the features of clothes?

Vocabulary

English: *bigger, smaller, equal, measure*

Spanish: *más grande, más pequeño, igual, medida*

Large Group

Opening Routine

• Sing a welcome song and talk about who's here.

Game: Finding Shapes on Clothing

• Review Mighty Minutes 20, "I Can Make a Circle." Follow the guidance on the card.

Discussion and Shared Writing: Looking at Large Clothes

• Introduce the visitor to the children or have the related child introduce the visitor.

• Ask the visitor to show the clothing that he brought to share.

• Ask him about the size of his clothes and refer to the list of questions the children generated yesterday.

• Allow children to ask their questions and compare their clothing sizes to his.

• If the visitor brought a baby picture, have him share it with the children. Compare the clothing in the picture with the size of clothing he wears now.

• Have the children measure the visitor's clothes with standard measuring tools, e.g., rulers or tape measure, and–or nonstandard tools, e.g., interlocking cubes or paper clips.

• Record children's comments and observations.

• Talk about the question of the day. "Do you see any shapes on our visitor's clothes?"

> Take photos of classroom visitors and children's investigations so you can document their learning and refer to those pictures throughout the study. Write a descriptive sentence underneath each one.

Before transitioning to interest areas, talk about the props from *Goldilocks and the Three Bears* that are in the Library area and how children may use them.

Choice Time

As you interact with children in the interest areas, make time to

- Observe each child's ability to recall the events of the story. Pay attention to how they negotiate roles and interact with each other during the retelling.

English-language learners
To help children who lack oral proficiency in English participate in dramatic play, model the language used for various roles so that children become familiar with it.

Read-Aloud

Read *A Pocket for Corduroy.*

- **Before you read**, share the title of the book and ask, "What do you think this book will be about?"

- **As you read**, ask, "Do you have pockets on your clothes? Why are they important?"

- **After you read**, help children review their predictions of what they thought the story would be about.

Small Group

Option 1: Bigger Than, Smaller Than, Equal To

- Review Intentional Teaching Card M09, "Bigger Than, Smaller Than, Equal To." Follow the guidance on the card.

Option 2: Measure & Compare

Review Intentional Teaching Card M12, "Measure & Compare." Follow the guidance on the card for measuring clothing items from the collection.

Mighty Minutes™

- Use Mighty Minutes 27, "Diddle, Diddle, Dumpling."

Large-Group Roundup

- Recall the day's events.
- Remind children that a baby is coming to visit the classroom tomorrow. Ask the children to think about questions that they would like to ask the caregiver about the baby's clothing. Record their questions.

What are the features of clothes?

Vocabulary

English: *nervous*

Spanish: *nervioso*

Large Group

Opening Routine

- Sing a welcome song and talk about who's here.

Rhyme: "Riddle Dee Dee"

- Review Mighty Minutes 04, "Riddle Dee Dee." Follow the guidance on the card.

Discussion and Shared Writing: Baby Visit

- Introduce the family member and baby to the children.

- Explain to the group that babies can be scared by loud voices so it is important that they use quiet voices when talking while the baby is in the classroom.

> At the beginning of an event or activity, talk to the children about how they should behave. This prepares them for success and reduces the likelihood of behavioral problems.

- Explain that some babies feel nervous if too many people touch them. Tell the children that before they touch the visiting baby, it is important to ask the baby's caregiver whether it is all right to touch the baby.

- Invite the family member to describe the clothing the baby wears.

- Have the family member show examples of clothing the baby wore as a newborn. Compare those clothing samples to the size the baby wears now, the children's clothing, and the shirt brought in yesterday by the male family member.

- Record children's ideas and take photos of the event.

Before transitioning to interest areas, talk about the baby clothes and measurement tools in the Toys and Games area and how children can use them.

Choice Time

As you interact with children in the interest areas, make time to

- Listen to their conversations as they measure the baby clothes.

- Ask questions, such as, "Which is bigger? How do you know? How many cubes long do you think that one is? How can you find out whether your guess is right?"

Read-Aloud

Read *Button, Button, Who's Got the Button?*

- **Before you read**, share the title of the book and ask, "What do you think the book will be about?"

- **As you read**, count objects in the book from a few chosen pages.

- **After you read**, ask, "How many buttons do you have on your clothes?" Assist the children with counting if needed.

Tell the children that the book will be available to them on the computer in the Computer area.

English-language learners
Count in children's home languages as well as in English. This provides opportunities for English-language learners to feel included and introduces other languages to all of the children.

Small Group

Option 1: Small, Medium, and Large Book

- Use Intentional Teaching Card LL04, "Bookmaking," and follow the guidance on the card.

- Help children recall the discussions about clothing sizes.

- Invite children to think about other things that come in small, medium, and large sizes to represent in their book.

Option 2: Small, Medium, and Large Computer Book

- Use Intentional Teaching Card LL02, "Desktop Publishing." Follow the guidance on the card.

- Have the children take digital photos of small, medium, and large items to use in making the book.

Mighty Minutes™

- Use Mighty Minutes 74, "Jack in the Box."

Large-Group Roundup

- Recall the day's events.
- Invite children to share the books made during small-group time.

Day 5 Investigation 1

What are the features of clothes?

Vocabulary

See Book Discussion Card 02, *The Mitten (El mitón)*, for words.

Large Group

Opening Routine

- Sing a welcome song and talk about who's here.

Music: Drums

- Use a real drum to demonstrate how a drum can be played, e.g., loud versus soft, fast versus slowly.

- Talk about the difference between just making noise and making music.

- Explain to children that in many places people don't use fancy instruments. They make music with the things around them.

- Give each child a common household item or allow them to find something in the room that can be used as a drum.

- Teach them how to hold the instrument in a resting position until everyone is ready.

- Play the beat to a familiar tune and invite the children to play along.

> When you teach children to hold the drum in a resting position, you are helping them control their impulse to beat it. Controlling impulses is part of self-regulation.

Discussion and Shared Writing: How do clothes stay on our bodies?

- Show the children a shirt and pants with buttons.

- Tell the children that buttons help us keep clothes on our bodies. Review the question of the day to see how many buttons the children can find on their clothes.

- Ask, "What else helps clothes stay on our bodies?"

- Record their responses on chart paper or a chalkboard.

Before transitioning to interest areas, talk about materials in the Art area that can be used to make thank-you notes for the family members who visited the class.

> Writing thank-you notes teaches children social skills and helps them understand that print is used to convey a message.

Choice Time

As you interact with children in the interest areas, make time to

- Record their dictation on the thank-you notes.

- Encourage them to do as much writing as they can, including signing their own names.

Read-Aloud

Read *The Mitten*.

- Use Book Discussion Card 02, "The Mitten." Follow the guidance on the card for the first read-aloud.

Small Group

Option 1: Tallying Features of Clothing

- Review Intentional Teaching Card M06, "Tallying."

- Invite the children to think of categories for the types of features that they would like to count, e.g., buttons, zippers, laces, drawstrings, and Velcro®.

Option 2: How Clothes Stay on Our Bodies

- Review Intentional Teaching Card M11, "Graphing."

- Have children examine their own clothing. Chart their ideas about the features that keep clothes on their bodies.

- Have some of the items they suggest available for them to explore, e.g., pieces of Velcro®, elastic, buttons, zippers, snaps, and laces.

- Follow the guidance on the card, basing categories on the clothing features the children identified, e.g., buttons, snaps, and so on.

Mighty Minutes™

- Use Mighty Minutes 25, "Freeze." Try the letter variation on the back of the card.

Large-Group Roundup

- Recall the day's events.

- Invite children to share their findings from their small-group work with the rest of the class.

Investigation 2

How do we take care of our clothes?

	Day 1	Day 2	Day 3
Interest Areas	**Sand and Water:** powder, liquid, and bar soaps; egg beaters; whisks **Dramatic Play:** laundry baskets **Computer:** eBook version of *Wash and Dry*	**Sand and Water:** soap, mixers, and beaters from the previous day's experience	**Library:** letter stamps **Art:** pieces of paper with a variety of lines drawn on them, e.g., straight, zigzag, curved; one or two lines per sheet
Question of the Day	Which soap will make the best bubbles: liquid, powder, or bar?	Which soap will clean best: liquid, powder, or bar?	Can you find something with a straight line and something with a curved line in our classroom?
Large Group	**Music:** Beating Drum Patterns **Discussion and Shared Writing:** Cleaning Clothes **Materials:** drums or objects to be used as drums; stained or dirty piece of clothing; Mighty Minutes 26, "Echo Clapping"; *Wash and Dry;* washboard; Intentional Teaching Card SE01, "Site Visits"	**Movement:** Move Like a Washer or Dryer **Discussion and Shared Writing:** Remembering a Trip to the Laundromat or read *Wash and Dry* **Materials:** *Wash and Dry;* a clothesline and clothespins for hanging clothes to dry.	**Song:** "This Is the Way We Wash Our Clothes" **Discussion and Shared Writing:** Finding and Making Lines **Materials:** Mighty Minutes 06, "This Is the Way"; clothesline
Read-Aloud	*The Mitten* Book Discussion Card 02 (second read-aloud)	*Llama Llama Red Pajama*	*The Mitten* Book Discussion Card 02 (third read-aloud)
Small Group	**Option 1: Letter Stamps** Intentional Teaching Card LL07, "Letters, Letters, Letters"; alphabet stamps; ink pads; construction paper or magnetic letters and board **Option 2: Shaving Cream Letters** Intentional Teaching Card LL13, "Shaving Cream Letters"; shaving cream	**Option 1: Button Letters** Intentional Teaching Card LL03, "Alphabet Cards"; buttons; alphabet cards **Option 2: Feeling Letters** Intentional Teaching Card LL15, "Texture Letters"; letters cut out of a variety of fabrics	**Option 1: Observing Changes** Intentional Teaching Card M07, "Ice Cubes"; ice cubes; paper towels; cups; measuring tools **Option 2: Baggie Ice Cream** Intentional Teaching Card M08, "Baggie Ice Cream" (See card for equipment, ingredients, and recipe.)
Mighty Minutes™	Mighty Minutes 53, "Three Rowdy Children"	Mighty Minutes 22, "Hot or Cold Shapes"; variety of three-dimensional shapes	Mighty Minutes 19, "I Spy With My Little Eye"

Day 4	Make Time For...

Library: clothesline story and props or the pocket storytelling props

Computer: eBook version of *Wash and Dry*

Do you have pockets on your clothes today?

Book: *A Pocket for Corduroy*

Discussion and Shared Writing: Mending

Materials: Mighty Minutes 04, "Riddle Dee Dee"; *A Pocket for Corduroy;* torn clothing; mending items, e.g., patches, zipper, Velcro®, button with needle and thread

Wash and Dry

Option 1: Dramatic Story Retelling

Intentional Teaching Card LL06, "Dramatic Story Retelling"; *The Mitten;* story props

Option 2: Pocket Storytelling

Intentional Teaching Card LL09, "Pocket Storytelling: *The Mitten*"; mitten-shaped pocket; toy or picture props

Mighty Minutes 13, "Simon Says"

Outdoor Experiences

Walking the Line

- Make long lines outside with masking tape or sidewalk chalk.

- Demonstrate how children can walk on them, e.g., when they walk on the straight line, tell them to keep their bodies straight; on curved lines, they should walk with a curved back, etc.

Going on a Line Hunt

- Invite children to look for various lines outside. Use a digital camera to take photos or let the children take pictures of the lines they find.

- Create a book of lines by using the photos the children took or download them onto a classroom computer for children to look at.

Family Partnerships

- Ask family members to accompany the class on the site visit.

- Invite a family member who sews to visit the class during Investigation 3, "How do people make clothes?"

- Invite families to access the eBook, *Wash and Dry*.

Wow! Experiences

- Day 1: Visit to a laundromat

When you call to schedule the site visit, talk with the manager to arrange for the children to interview a staff member if possible.

How do we take care of our clothes?

Vocabulary

English: *powder, liquid, solid, laundromat*

Spanish: *polvo, líquido, en barra, lavandería*

See Book Discussion Card 02, *The Mitten (El mitón)*, for additional words.

Large Group

Opening Routine

- Sing a welcome song and talk about who's here.

Music: Beating Drum Patterns

- Give each child a drum or common household object or allow them to find something in the room that can be used as a drum.

- Remind the children how to hold the instrument in a resting position until everyone is ready.

- Review Mighty Minutes Card 26, "Echo Clapping."

- Follow the guidance on the card using drums.

Discussion and Shared Writing: Cleaning Clothes

- Show a clothing item that is obviously dirty. Ask, "What do you think I need to do to get this clean?"

- After children share ideas, explain, "People wash clothes in many ways."

- Read the book, *Wash and Dry*.

- If possible, bring in a washboard to demonstrate how it is used.

- If you are planning a site visit, ask, "Do you know the name of a place with many washers and dryers in one room?" Introduce the term *laundromat*.

- Ask, "What do you think you might see there? What would you like to ask the person who works at the laundromat?" Record their questions.

Before transitioning to interest areas, talk about the different kinds of soap (*powder, liquid*, and *solid bar*), the mixers at the water table, and the laundry baskets in the Dramatic Play area and how children can use them.

English-language learners
Show children an example of each type of soap as you name it.

Before the site visit, remind children about expectations. (See Intentional Teaching Card SE01, "Site Visit," for more information.)

Choice Time

As you interact with children in the interest areas, make time to

- Observe the children making bubbles.

- Review the question of the day and check their predictions.

- Describe the process of separating light- and dark-colored clothing before washing them. Invite children to sort clothes using the baskets in the Dramatic Play area.

Read-Aloud

Read *The Mitten.*

- Use Book Discussion Card 02, "The Mitten." Follow the guidance for the second read-aloud.

Small Group

Option 1: Letter Stamps

- Review Intentional Teaching Card LL07, "Letters, Letters, Letters." Follow the guidance on the card.

Option 2: Shaving Cream Letters

- Review Intentional Teaching Card LL13, "Shaving Cream Letters." Follow the guidance on the card.

> Providing children with multiple ways to explore the alphabet helps them begin to recognize and name letters.

Mighty Minutes™

- Use Mighty Minutes 53, "Three Rowdy Children."

Large-Group Roundup

- Recall the day's events.

- Explain, "Tomorrow we will predict and test which type of soap will clean clothes best. Ask your family members which kind they think cleans best: *powder*, *liquid*, or bar soap."

Investigation 2

How do we take care of our clothes?

Vocabulary

English: *laundromat, clothesline, powder, liquid, solid*

Spanish: *lavandería, cuerda para secar ropa, polvo, líquido, en barra*

Large Group

Opening Routine

- Sing a welcome song and talk about who's here.

Movement: Move Like a Washer and Dryer

- Say to the children, "We are going to create our own pretend laundromat with our bodies. Let's think about the movements and sounds a washer and dryer make. Today we will be the machines."

- Have children keep their feet in one place while creatively moving their bodies rhythmically like the washing machine.

- Encourage them to make various rhythmic sounds. Repeat with twisting and turning motions and dryer sounds.

- Take turns pressing the pretend buttons, putting in the coins, and turning on some or all of the machines.

Discussion and Shared Writing: Remembering a Trip to the Laundromat

- Recall the site visit from yesterday.

- Show the pages of *Wash and Dry* that describe the laundromat. If children visited the *laundromat*, compare their experience to the book. Record their observations.

Before transitioning to interest areas, talk about cleaning the dirty clothes and the three kinds of soap (*powder, liquid*, and *solid bar*) at the water table. Demonstrate the process of hanging clean clothes to dry on a *clothesline*. If you do not have easy access to the outdoors from your classroom, or if it is too cold, hang the clothesline inside near the Sand and Water area, and put towels on the floor under the line to catch any drips of water.

Choice Time

As you interact with children in the interest areas, make time to

- Observe children as they experiment with the soaps. Encourage them to record their findings again on the question-of-the-day chart.

- Describe how the *solid* bar of soap gets soft and eventually changes state after being left in water for a while.

> **Experimenting with bar, liquid, and powdered soap helps children gain an understanding of the physical properties of objects as well as how objects change. These are important scientific concepts.**

Read-Aloud

Read *Llama Llama Red Pajama*.

- **Before you read**, remind children that the little llama wears red pajamas for bedtime. Ask, "What do you wear at bedtime?" Record their responses.

- **As you read**, pause, allowing children to fill in some of the rhyming words.

- **After you read**, look through the pages of the book and talk about baby llama's bedtime routine (reads a book with mama, has a stuffed animal he holds, gets kisses, asks for a drink). Invite children to describe their bedtime routines. Ask, "What do you do before you go to sleep at night?"

Small Group

Option 1: Button Letters

- Review Intentional Teaching Card LL03, "Alphabet Cards." Follow the guidance on the card using buttons to form the letters.

Option 2: Feeling Letters

- Review Intentional Teaching Card LL15, "Texture Letters." Follow the guidance on the card using different fabrics to make the letters.

Mighty Minutes™

- Use Mighty Minutes 22, "Hot or Cold Shapes."

Large-Group Roundup

- Recall the day's events.

- Discuss the question of the day and how children's predictions at the beginning of the day compare with their findings during choice time.

- Write a group thank-you note to the owner of the laundromat. Invite the children to add drawings and to write their names on the note.

Day 3 Investigation 2

How do we take care of our clothes?

Vocabulary

English: *straight, curve, slant*

Spanish: *recta, curva, inclinada*

See Book Discussion Card 02, *The Mitten (El mitón)*, for additional words.

Large Group

Opening Routine

- Sing a welcome song and talk about who's here.

Song: "This Is the Way We Wash Our Clothes"

- Review Mighty Minutes 06, "This Is the Way."

- Adapt the song to include "…wash our clothes," "…dry our clothes," "…hang our clothes," and "…fold our clothes."

English-language learners
Observe English-language learners carefully when the class is singing together. Children who have not previously spoken English around others often begin using the language for the first time when singing with a group.

Discussion and Shared Writing: Finding and Making Lines

- Show the clothesline the children used yesterday and remind them how to use it.

- Ask, "Where are other places you can find lines?"

- Remind children about the question of the day.

- Have children find something in the room with a straight or curved line. Explain that some straight lines go up and down and some go from side to side. Sometimes a straight line is slanted; it leans to the side.

- Record the places they find lines, e.g., "The round table has a *curved* line."

- Tell them, "We can also make lines with our bodies."

- Invite children to stand or lie down and make various kinds of lines with their bodies.

Before transitioning to interest areas, talk about the letter stamps and the paper with lines to cut along and how children can use them in the Art area.

Choice Time	As you interact with children in the interest areas, make time to • Observe their ability to cut along the different lines.	• Note how children use the letter stamps. Are they stamping randomly on the page, or do they stamp from left to right as in reading and writing? Also note which letters children can identify correctly and whether they try to spell anything with the letters.
Read-Aloud	Read *The Mitten*. • Use Book Discussion Card 02, "The Mitten." Follow the guidance for the third read-aloud.	
Small Group	**Option 1: Observing Changes** • Review Intentional Teaching Card M07, "Ice Cubes." Follow the guidance on the card to observe an ice cube melt.	**Option 2: Baggie Ice Cream** • Review Intentional Teaching Card M08, "Baggie Ice Cream." Follow the guidance on the card.
Mighty Minutes™	Use Mighty Minutes 19, "I Spy With My Little Eye." Use the beginning sound variation on the card.	
Large-Group Roundup	• Recall the day's events. • Ask children who worked on cutting lines to talk about their experiences. Ask, "Which lines were easiest to cut? Which were hardest? Why?"	

Day 4   Investigation 2

How do we take care of our clothes?

Vocabulary

English: *mend*

Spanish: *arreglar*

Large Group

Opening Routine

- Sing a welcome song and talk about who's here.

Rhyme: "Riddle Dee Dee"

- Review Mighty Minutes Card 04, "Riddle Dee Dee." Follow the guidance on the card.

Discussion and Shared Writing: Mending

- Review the question of the day.

- Read *A Pocket for Corduroy*. Discuss how the character, Lisa, makes a pocket for Corduroy.

- Show the children a piece of torn clothing and ask them whether they have ever had a tear in their clothing.

- Ask, "What would you do if your clothes tore and needed to be *mended*?"

- Explain the term *mend*. Show a couple of items that you might use while mending clothing, e.g., a patch, a zipper, Velcro®, a button, a needle, and thread.

- Encourage the children to explore the materials and ask questions about them.

Before transitioning to interest areas, tell the children that *Wash and Dry* will be available on the computer in the Computer area.

> **See Intentional Teaching Card LL43, "Introducing New Vocabulary," for ideas on expanding children's vocabularies.**

Choice Time

As you interact with children in the interest areas, make time to

- Observe their ability to recall and retell the events of the story.

- Observe children using the computer. Offer assistance if necessary.

Read-Aloud

Read *Wash and Dry*.

- **Before you read**, share the title of the book.

- **As you read**, ask, "Is this how you wash your clothes at home?"

- **After you read**, list all of the ways that people washed clothes in the book across the top of a piece of chart paper. Invite children to write their names under the method that they use at home with their families to wash their clothes. Discuss the chart, e.g., four children go to the laundromat to wash clothes and six children use a washing machine at their homes.

Small Group

Option 1: Dramatic Story Retelling

- Review Intentional Teaching Card LL06, "Dramatic Story Retelling." Follow the guidance on the card using *The Mitten*.

Option 2: Pocket Storytelling

- Review Intentional Teaching Card LL09, "Pocket Storytelling: *The Mitten*." Follow the guidance on the card.

Mighty Minutes™

- Use Mighty Minutes 13, "Simon Says." Try using two- and three-step directions while you play.

Large-Group Roundup

- Recall the day's events.
- Ask children to share their observations about their small-group experience.

Investigation 3

How do people make clothes?

	Day 1	Day 2	Day 3
Interest Areas	Art: materials for designing shirts: pencils, paper, stamps, stencils, rulers, markers	Toys and Games: fabric scraps cut into pieces to match or pattern Art: large paper for body tracings Computer: eBook version of *The Quinceañera*	Toys and Games: geoboards; geobands Dramatic Play: fabric pieces that can be draped or tied to create clothes Art: large paper for body tracing
Question of the Day	What is written on your clothes: words, numbers, or nothing?	Do you think we can we make clothes?	What colors mix together to make green?
Large Group	Game: Sort by Shirt Design Discussion and Shared Writing: Designing Clothes (show sketch in *The Quinceañera*) Materials: digital camera; *The Quinceañera*	Book: *The Quinceañera* Discussion and Shared Writing: Do You Think We Can Make Clothes? Materials: *The Quinceañera*	Movement: Making Shapes With Scarves Discussion and Shared Writing: Visitor Who Sews Materials: scarves; shape cards; music; digital camera
Read-Aloud	*The Girl Who Wore Too Much* Book Discussion Card 03 (first read-aloud)	*Something From Nothing*	*The Girl Who Wore Too Much* Book Discussion Card 03 (second read-aloud)
Small Group	Option 1: Patterns on Clothing Intentional Teaching Card M14, "Patterns"; clothing collection; crayons, markers, or pencils; paper Option 2: Button Patterns Intentional Teaching Card M14, "Patterns"; buttons; crayons, markers, or pencils; paper	Option 1: Sewing Paper Intentional Teaching Card P01, "Let's Sew"; hole punch; yarn; toothpicks; heavyweight paper Option 2: Let's Sew Intentional Teaching Card P01, "Let's Sew"; burlap or other loosely woven fabric or plastic mesh; blunt needles; yarn or thick thread	Option 1: Mixing Paints Intentional Teaching Card P30, "Mixing Paints"; red, blue, yellow, black, and white paints; tray; paintbrushes; paper; *The Girl Who Wore Too Much*; *The Quinceañera* Option 2: Dyeing Paper Towels Intentional Teaching Card P31, "Tie-Dyed Towels"; paper towels; food coloring; eye droppers; ice cube tray; clothespins; clothesline; *The Girl Who Wore Too Much*
Mighty Minutes™	Mighty Minutes 16, "Nothing, Nothing, Something"	Mighty Minutes 12, "Ticky Ricky"	Mighty Minutes 24, "Dinky Doo"

	Day 4	Day 5	Make Time For...
	Art: large paper for body tracing Library: materials for thank-you notes	Art Area: fabric scraps; glue Toys and Games: matching fabric scraps	**Outdoor Experiences** **Follow the Leader on a Line** • Make long lines with masking tape or sidewalk chalk outside. • Lead a game of follow the leader, having children move in different ways along different lines, e.g., skip on the curved line, hop on the straight line, and gallop on the zigzag line. • Invite children to take turns leading.
	Which fabric pattern do you like best? (Display different fabric patterns.)	What kind of clothes will you design today?	
	Movement: Body Lines Discussion and Shared Writing: Thinking About Lines Materials: Mighty Minutes 09, "Writing in the Air"	Book: *Something From Nothing* Discussion and Shared Writing: Using Fabric Pieces to Make Clothes Materials: *Something From Nothing*; *A Pocket for Corduroy*; fabric scraps	**Physical Fun** • Intentional Teaching Card P09, "Up and Away." **Family Partnerships** • Invite a family member who knits or crochets to visit the class during Investigation 4, "How is cloth made?" • Invite families to access the eBook, *The Quinceañera*.
	Abuela's Weave	*The Girl Who Wore Too Much* Book Discussion Card 03 (third read-aloud)	**Wow! Experiences** • Day 3: A visit from someone who sews
	Option 1: Writing Poetry Intentional Teaching Card LL27, "Writing Poems"; audio recorder Option 2: A Collection of Poems Intentional Teaching Card LL27, "Writing Poems"; audio recorder; digital camera	Option 1: Writing Poetry Intentional Teaching Card LL27, "Writing Poems"; audio recorder Option 2: A Collection of Poems Intentional Teaching Card LL27, "Writing Poems"; audio recorder; digital camera	
	Mighty Minutes 28, "Counting Calisthenics"	Mighty Minutes 42, "Come Play With Me"	

How do people make clothes?

Vocabulary

English: *sketch, design, fashion designer*

Spanish: *boceto, diseño, diseñador(a) de modas*

See Book Discussion Card 03, *The Girl Who Wore Too Much* (*La joven que tenía demasiado*), for additional words.

Large Group

Opening Routine

- Sing a welcome song and talk about who's here.

Game: Sort by Shirt Design

- Remind children about the question of the day. Invite them to describe what is on their clothes.

- Help children sort themselves by categories, e.g., shirts with words, shirts with decorations, shirts with polka dots.

- Take a photo of the children organized in categories for a display or class book.

Discussion and Shared Writing: Designing Clothes

- Tell children that people who design clothes have to first *sketch* or draw them before they can make them.

- Show children the page from *The Quinceañera* that illustrates a sketch of the clothing before it is made.

- Explain, "People whose job it is to *design* clothes are called *fashion designers*."

- Ask, "If you could *design* a shirt, what would it look like?"

- Record their responses.

Before transitioning to interest areas, explain to the children that they will get the chance to be fashion designers. Show the materials in the Art area that they can use to design a shirt.

Choice Time

As you interact with children in the interest areas, make time to

- Ask children about their designs and record what they say on another sheet of paper.

> Create a display of the shirts and the children's descriptions to show them that you value their work and give them an opportunity to view each other's designs.

Read-Aloud	Read *The Girl Who Wore Too Much*.	
	• Use Book Discussion Card 03, "The Girl Who Wore Too Much." Follow the guidance for the first read-aloud.	

Small Group	**Option 1: Patterns on Clothing**	**Option 2: Button Patterns**
	• Review Intentional Teaching Card M14, "Patterns."	• Review Intentional Teaching Card M14, "Patterns."
	• Use the clothing collection to help children identify patterns on the fabrics.	• Follow the guidance on the card to have children create patterns using buttons.
	• Invite the children to record their observations on paper using crayons, markers, and pencils and to create new patterns.	

Mighty Minutes™	• Use Mighty Minutes 16, "Nothing, Nothing, Something." Try making all of the imagined objects begin with the same letter sound.

Large-Group Roundup	• Recall the day's events. • Invite children to share their shirt designs with the group.

How do people make clothes?

Vocabulary

English: *seamstress, tailors, stitch, hem, sewing machine, manufactured*

Spanish: *costurera, sastres, puntada, ruedo, máquina de coser, manufacturado*

Large Group

Opening Routine

- Sing a welcome song and talk about who's here.

Book: *The Quinceañera*

- Read the book to the children, pausing to explain new vocabulary words: *seamstress, tailors, stitch, hem, sewing machine, manufactured.*

Discussion and Shared Writing: Do You Think We Can Make Clothes?

- Tell the children that not all clothes are sewn. Tell them that sometimes pieces of fabric are draped to make clothes.

- Demonstrate draping by taking a large piece of fabric and wrapping it around your body like a shawl, sari, or sarong.

- Refer to the question of the day. Ask, "Do you think we can make clothes? What will we need? What kinds of things can we use to make clothes?"

- Record children's ideas.

- Tell the children that tomorrow you will have some of the materials they suggested available during choice time and that today, in small groups, they will have the opportunity to practice sewing.

Before transitioning to interest areas, talk about the fabric scraps in the Toys and Games area for matching and pattern making. Tell the children that you will help trace around their bodies on big paper in the Art area and then cut out the shape. Tell the children that *The Quinceañera* will be available on the computer in the Computer area.

Choice Time

As you interact with children in the interest areas, make time to

- Observe their ability to match fabrics that are alike. Ask about the patterns they create.

- Trace around a few children's bodies and have children help cut out the tracings.

Read-Aloud

Read *Something From Nothing*.

- **Before you read**, show the cover. Ask, "What do you think this story is about?" Explain, "Pay attention to what is happening in the illustrations as we read the story."

- **As you read**, pause occasionally, encouraging the children to look at the details in the illustrations.

- **After you read**, look back through the illustrations and discuss the process that the grandfather uses to sew things.

Small Group

Option 1: Sewing Paper

- Review Intentional Teaching Card P01, "Let's Sew." Follow the guidance on the card using paper and toothpicks.

Option 2: Let's Sew

- Review Intentional Teaching Card P01, "Let's Sew." Follow the guidance on the card using burlap and thick sewing needles instead of paper and toothpicks.

> Sewing builds many fine-motor skills necessary for writing. Children have to hold the needle and use eye–hand coordination to make the needle go through the hole. They must also remember how to guide the needle in and out of the fabric.

Mighty Minutes™

- Use Mighty Minutes 12, "Ticky Ricky."

- As you say the rhyme, either tap, clap, snap, or stomp a pattern, e.g., stomp, stomp, clap; stomp, stomp, clap.

Large-Group Roundup

- Recall the day's events.

- Invite children to share their sewing projects with the rest of the group.

- Remind the children that a visitor is coming tomorrow to demonstrate sewing. On chart paper, record the questions children would like to ask the visitor.

Day 3 Investigation 3

How do people make clothes?

Vocabulary

See Book Discussion Card 03, *The Girl Who Wore Too Much*
(*La joven que tenía demasiado*), for words.

Large Group

Opening Routine

- Sing a welcome song and talk about who's here.

Movement: Making Shapes With Scarves

- Give each child a scarf.

- Play music and encourage children to move their bodies and the scarves to the music.

- Next, show the children a shape card and ask them to make the shape shown on the card using their scarves.

- Assist children, as needed, encouraging them to partner to help one another.

Discussion and Shared Writing: Visitor Who Sews

- Introduce the visitor to the class.

- Have the visitor show the different tools he or she uses to make clothes, e.g., sewing machine, needle and thread, pin cushion, patterns.

- Take photos of each step to refer to later in the clothes-making experience.

- Invite the children to ask questions.

- Record the responses.

Before transitioning to interest areas, talk about the fabric available in the Dramatic Play area and geobands to create straight, curved, and zigzag lines in the Toys and Games area.

Choice Time

As you interact with children in the interest areas, make time to

- Observe children as they use the materials in the Dramatic Play area.

- Talk to children about their geoboard creations.

- Take photos of children in their draped clothing creations.

- Trace around a few children's bodies and have children help cut out the tracings.

Read-Aloud

Read *The Girl Who Wore Too Much.*

- Use Book Discussion Card 03, "The Girl Who Wore Too Much." Follow the guidance for the second read-aloud.

Small Group

Option 1: Mixing Paints

- Review Intentional Teaching Card P30, "Mixing Paints."

- Look back through *The Girl Who Wore Too Much.* With the children, identify the colors named in the book. List them on a piece of paper.

- Follow the guidance on the card to mix paint colors to make the colors in the book.

- When finished, encourage children to arrange the paper they painted on from darkest to lightest.

- Refer to the question of the day.

Option 2: Dyeing Paper Towels

- Review Intentional Teaching Card P31, "Tie-Dyed Towels."

- Look back through *The Girl Who Wore Too Much.* With the children, identify the colors named in the book. List them on a piece of paper.

- Follow the guidance on the card to mix colors to make the colors in the book.

- When finished, encourage children to arrange the colored paper towels from darkest to lightest.

- Refer to the question of the day as children experiment with the colors.

Mighty Minutes™

- Use Mighty Minutes 24, "Dinky Doo."

Large-Group Roundup

- Recall the day's events.
- Invite children to share their color-mixing work with the group.

- Show the photos of children wearing draped clothing. Invite the children to talk about their experiences.

How do people make clothes?

Vocabulary

English: *huipil, tapestry*

Spanish: *huipil, tapiz*

Large Group

Opening Routine

- Sing a welcome song and talk about who's here.

Movement: Body Lines

- Review Mighty Minutes 09, "Writing in the Air." Follow the guidance on the card.

Discussion and Shared Writing: Thinking About Lines

- Review the question of the day.

- Draw a simple sketch of an article of clothing and remind children that clothing has straight lines and curved lines. Sometimes the straight lines go up and down; sometimes they go from side to side. Other straight lines are slanted and look like they are leaning.

- Show a few samples of clothing with lines.

- Briefly relate the idea of lines to letters. Some have straight lines, some have curved lines, and some have slanted lines.

- Have children search the room for letters with each kind of line.

> Write examples of the letters as you discuss their lines. For example, you might say as you make a *D*, "The letter *D* has both a straight line and a curved line."

Before transitioning to interest areas, talk about the materials in the Library area for writing thank-you notes.

Choice Time

As you interact with children in the interest areas, make time to

- Record their dictation on the cards. Invite them to do as much writing as they can, including signing their own names.

- In the Art area, trace around a few children's bodies and have them help cut out the tracings.

Read-Aloud

Read *Abuela's Weave*.

- **Before you read**, tell children the name of the book and show the book cover. Invite the children to describe the illustration. Ask, "What do you think this story is about?"

- **As you read**, comment on how Esperanza was worried that no one would buy the *huipiles* and *tapestries* that she and her grandmother made. Briefly define *huipil* and *tapestry*.

- **After you read**, ask, "Did you ever work hard to make something beautiful? How did you feel when you were done? How did you feel when you showed it to someone else?"

Small Group

Option 1: Writing Poetry

- Review Intentional Teaching Card LL27, "Writing Poems."

- Read the following poem:

  When I run with my pet,
  My sock gets wet.
  I don't know what to do.
  Now I see that other kids
  Don't take off their shoe.

- Read the other examples of poetry on the card or share other poems you have in the classroom.

- Follow the guidance on the card to help children create their own poetry about an item from the clothing collection.

Option 2: A Collection of Poems

- Review Intentional Teaching Card LL27, "Writing Poems."

- Read the following poem:

  When I run with my pet,
  My sock gets wet.
  I don't know what to do.
  Now I see that other kids
  Don't take off their shoe.

- Read the other examples of poetry on the card or share other poems you have in the classroom.

- Follow the guidance on the card to help children create their own poetry about an item from the clothing collection.

- Take photos of the children wearing the clothing item and display them next to the poems.

Mighty Minutes™

- Use Mighty Minutes 28, "Counting Calisthenics." Follow the guidance on the card.

Large-Group Roundup

- Recall the day's events.

- Invite the children who worked on creating poetry to share their work.

Investigation 3

How do people make clothes?

Vocabulary

See Book Discussion Card 03, *The Girl Who Wore Too Much*
(*La joven que tenía demasiado*), for words.

Large Group

Opening Routine

- Sing a welcome song and talk about who's here.

Book: *Something From Nothing*

- Reread the book and draw children's attention to the ways they have made clothes this week and how the visitor made clothes.

Discussion and Shared Writing: Using Fabric Pieces to Make Clothes

- Explain that another way to make clothes is to put different kinds of fabric pieces together.

- Show the illustrations in *A Pocket for Corduroy* and talk about how Lisa uses a scrap of fabric to make the pocket.

Before transitioning to interest areas, talk about the fabric scraps and glue in the Art area that the children can use to make clothes for their cut out bodies.

> **Digital photos of children's faces can be enlarged and glued on the body cutouts.**

Choice Time

As you interact with children in the interest areas, make time to

- Talk to them about their clothing creations. Say, "Tell me about the clothes you are designing."

- Record their responses on a different sheet of paper. Hang their descriptions next to their work.

- Remind children of the question of the day.

Read-Aloud	Read *The Girl Who Wore Too Much*. • Use Book Discussion Card 03, "The Girl Who Wore Too Much." Follow the guidance on the card for the third read-aloud.

Small Group

Option 1: Writing Poetry

- Review Intentional Teaching Card LL27, "Writing Poems."

- Read the following poem:

  When I run with my pet,
  My sock gets wet.
  I don't know what to do.
  Now I see that other kids
  Don't take off their shoe.

- Read the other examples of poetry on the card or share other poems you have in the classroom.

- Follow the guidance on the card to help children create their own poetry about an item from the clothing collection.

Option 2: A Collection of Poems

- Review Intentional Teaching Card LL27, "Writing Poems."

- Read the following poem:

  When I run with my pet,
  My sock gets wet.
  I don't know what to do.
  Now I see that other kids
  Don't take off their shoe.

- Read the other examples of poetry on the card or share other poems you have in the classroom.

- Follow the guidance on the card to help children create their own poetry about an item from the clothing collection.

- Take photos of the children wearing the clothing item and display them next to the poems.

> **When you repeat small group experiences several times, children can build on what they have learned.**

Mighty Minutes™

- Use Mighty Minutes 42, "Come Play With Me." Follow the guidance on the card.

Large-Group Roundup

- Recall the day's events.
- Walk around the room and look at each other's clothing creations for their body tracings.

Investigation 4

How is cloth made?

	Day 1	Day 2	Day 3
Interest Areas	**Discovery:** fabric; magnifying glasses; Intentional Teaching Card LL45, "Observational Drawing"; clipboards; felt-tip pens	**Art:** strips of paper for children to weave in and out of paper or cardboard; prepared paper for weaving **Library:** *Abuela's Weave*	**Discovery:** *The Quinceañera* **Dramatic Play:** class loom (See the directions for making a loom that are given on the next page.)
Question of the Day	What does the fabric on your shirt feel like?	What comes next in the pattern? (Display a simple repeating pattern, such as blue-red-blue-red.)	What comes from sheep?
Large Group	**Game:** Sorting Ourselves **Discussion and Shared Writing:** How Is Cloth Made? **Materials:** *The Quinceañera*; pieces of woven fabric	**Movement:** Body Weaving **Discussion and Shared Writing:** Weaving **Materials:** broom handles or yardsticks; crocheted or knitted clothing item or blanket; magnifying glasses	**Song:** "Baa, Baa, Black Sheep" **Discussion and Shared Writing:** How Cloth Is Made **Materials:** Mighty Minutes 29, "Baa, Baa, Black Sheep"; *The Quinceañera*; a piece of raw wool (if available); class loom; ribbon
Read-Aloud	*The Paper Bag Princess*	*Button, Button, Who's Got the Button?*	*Uncle Nacho's Hat*
Small Group	**Option 1: Playing With Print** Intentional Teaching Card LL23, "Playing With Environmental Print"; environmental print, e.g., cereal boxes; logos; stop signs **Option 2: Shopping Trip** Intentional Teaching Card LL31, "I Went Shopping"; environmental print found in a grocery store, e.g., empty product containers or labels; grocery bag	**Option 1: Geoboards** Intentional Teaching Card M21, "Geoboards"; geoboards; bands; shape cards **Option 2: I'm Thinking of a Shape** Intentional Teaching Card M20, "I'm Thinking of a Shape"; geometric solids; empty containers shaped like geometric solids	**Option 1: Play Dough Weaving** Intentional Teaching Card P02, "Play Dough Weaving"; play dough; play dough tools **Option 2: Twisted Pretzels** Intentional Teaching Card P03, "Twisted Pretzels" (See card for equipment, ingredients, and recipe.)
Mighty Minutes™	Mighty Minutes 19, "I Spy With My Little Eye"	Mighty Minutes 29, "Baa, Baa, Black Sheep"	Mighty Minutes 21, "Hully Gully, How Many?"

Make Time For…

Outdoor Experiences

Go In and Out the Windows

- Have the children stand in a circle holding hands, lifting them up in the air to form "windows." As you sing, invite one child to weave in and out the windows (your raised arms).

Physical Fun

- Intentional Teaching Card P10, "Jumping Rope"

Family Partnerships

- Inform families that the class will be conducting a clothing drive at the end of the study. Ask them to start collecting clothing to donate. You may also want to ask a few family members to help take the clothes to a donation site after the clothing drive.

Wow! Experiences

- Day 1: A visit from someone who knits or crochets

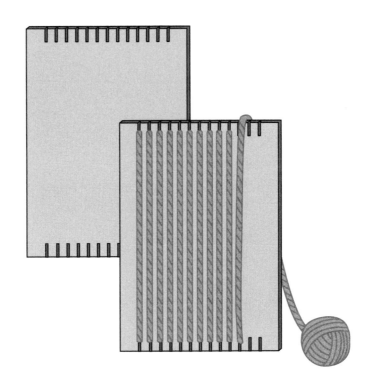

How to Make a Loom

Use a large cardboard rectangle and mark every ¼" on both the top and bottom. Make 1" cuts on each of the marks you measured, making sure that the bottom marks line up perfectly with the top marks (see picture above). String the warp or vertical yarns. Tie a large knot on the end of your string to hold the string in place. Slide the string into the first slot and gently pull until knot is secure. Pull the string tightly down the corresponding slot on the bottom and insert the string into this first slot. Tightly pull the string up the back and insert into the second top slot, and then down to the second bottom slot. Repeat procedure until all slots are full. Tie off the string and trim the excess (see picture).

How is cloth made?

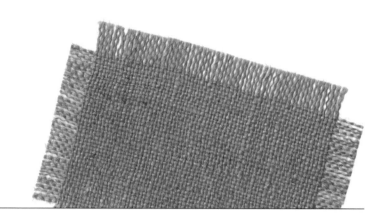

Vocabulary

English: *loom, weave, knit, crochet, cloth*

Spanish: *telar, entretejer, tejer, croché, tela*

Large Group

Opening Routine

- Sing a welcome song and talk about who's here.

Game: Sorting Ourselves

- Recall the question of the day. Invite the children to pick an item of clothing that they are wearing and feel it.

- Ask, "How does it feel?" If they need help, ask follow-up questions, such as, "Is it soft, rough, bumpy, or smooth?"

- Record their words on a chart.

- Have the children select a few descriptors and then sort themselves into groups, e.g., all the children with a bumpy clothing item would go into one group.

- Select new categories and have them resort themselves. If this is difficult for the children, choose only two categories at a time, e.g., bumpy and not bumpy.

English-language learners
When using the words *smooth*, *soft*, *bumpy*, and *rough* in questions, hold up samples of those textures and pass them around so that children can understand the meaning of these adjectives.

Discussion and Shared Writing: How Is Cloth Made?

- Ask, "How do you think cloth is made?"

- Introduce the invited family member or other volunteer to demonstrate how to knit or crochet.

- Show a picture of the loom from *The Quinceañera*. Explain that a loom is similar to crocheting or knitting, because it weaves threads to make cloth.

- Allow children to pass around and feel the textures of many types of woven fabric.

- Have children compare and contrast the fabric pieces. Record their ideas.

Giving children something to hold or pass around during large-group time keeps them actively involved and helps sustain their attention.

Before transitioning to interest areas, talk about the fabrics and magnifying glasses in the Discovery area and how children can use them.

Choice Time

As you interact with children in the interest areas, make time to

- Ask, "What do you see when you look at the fabric through the magnifying glass?"

- Invite them to record their observations.

See Intentional Teaching Card LL45, "Observational Drawing," for more information on supporting children's observational drawings.

Read-Aloud

Read *The Paper Bag Princess.*

- **Before you read**, read the title of the story. Say, "I wonder why this princess is wearing a paper bag."

- **As you read**, invite the children to make predictions about what will happen next.

- **After you read**, say, "Elizabeth made clothes out of a paper bag when the dragon burned all of her clothes. What would you make clothes out of if you lost yours?"

Small Group

Option 1: Playing with Print

- Review Intentional Teaching Card LL23, "Playing With Environmental Print."

- Follow the guidance on the card.

Option 2: Shopping Trip

- Review Intentional Teaching Card LL31, "I Went Shopping."

- Follow the guidance on the card.

Mighty Minutes™

- Use Mighty Minutes 19, "I Spy With My Little Eye."

- Try the beginning sound variation on the card.

Large-Group Roundup

- Recall the day's events.

- Shared writing: Write a group thank-you note to today's visitor.

Day 2   Investigation 4

How is cloth made?

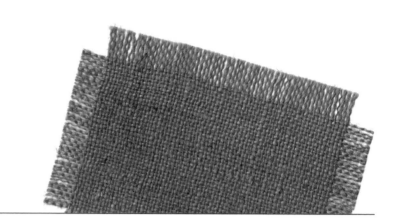

Vocabulary

English: *loom, weave, knit, crochet, cloth*

Spanish: *telar, entretejer, tejer, croché, tela*

Large Group

Opening Routine

- Sing a welcome song and talk about who's here.

Movement: Body Weaving

- Remind children of the new terms they learned about yesterday, e.g., *loom, weave, knit, crochet, cloth*.

- Tell them that today the class will be trying to weave.

- Talk about the question of the day and encourage them to say what comes next in the pattern.

- Demonstrate that the motion to create a weave is over-under-over-under.

- Create obstacles in the classroom for children to practice going over-under-over-under with their bodies. You can use yardsticks or a broom handle. Hold one high in the air, place one on the ground, and repeat the pattern.

- Have the children who are waiting call out the over-under pattern while one or two children at a time go through the motions.

This weaving activity teaches children two key skills. First, children learn about spatial awareness by connecting the concepts of over and under with movement. This is called *kinesthetic learning*. Second, they are making a pattern (over–under). Being able to identify and extend patterns is an important math skill that children will build on.

Discussion and Shared Writing: Weaving

- Show a sample of a crocheted or knitted blanket or clothing item.

- Distribute magnifying glasses so children can get a detailed look at the item.

- Ask the children to describe it. Record their descriptions.

Before transitioning to interest areas, talk about the weaving paper in the Art area and how the children can use the materials. Prepare the paper this way: Fold each piece of paper in half and make cuts about 1" apart on the folded side. Stop cutting about 1" before you reach the edge. When you open it, you'll have a paper with lines cut across it. Demonstrate how to weave paper strips over and under the larger paper (between the cuts).

Choice Time

As you interact with children in the interest areas, make time to

- Assist children as needed to weave paper.

- Model self-talk by repeating "Over-under-over-under."

- Read *Abuela's Weave*. Ask children how the loom pictured in the book is the same or different than the loom in *The Quinceañera*.

> **Self-talk is a strategy children can use to remember what to do and to process their experiences.**

Read-Aloud

Read *Button, Button, Who's Got the Button?*

- **Before you read**, ask, "What do you remember about this book?"

- **As you read**, invite children to point to the items and count them on each page.

- **After you read**, say, "I wonder which of the clothing features in the book we can find on our clothes." Review the items and encourage children to locate them on their own clothes.

Small Group

Option 1: Geoboards

- Review Intentional Teaching Card M21, "Geoboards."

- Have the children select a shape card from the stack.

- Follow the guidance on the card to encourage them to make the shape on the card.

Option 2: I'm Thinking of a Shape

- Review Intentional Teaching Card M20, "I'm Thinking of a Shape." Follow the guidance on the card.

Mighty Minutes™

- Use Mighty Minutes 29, "Baa, Baa, Black Sheep." Follow the guidance on the card.

Large-Group Roundup

- Recall the day's events.

- Invite children to share their weaving creations with the group.

Investigation 4

How is cloth made?

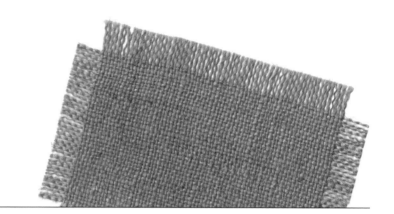

Vocabulary

English: *appreciate, decent*

Spanish: *apreciar, decente*

Large Group

Opening Routine

- Sing a welcome song and talk about who's here.

Song: "Baa, Baa, Black Sheep"

- Use Mighty Minutes 29, "Baa, Baa, Black Sheep."

- Write the words to the song on a chart.

- Display the chart.

- Invite children to point to the letter *B* or *b*.

> **"Baa, Baa, Black..." is an example of alliteration—a group of words all beginning with the same sound.**

Discussion and Shared Writing: How Cloth Is Made

- If available, share a piece of wool for children to examine.

- Review the question of the day.

- Refer to the end of *The Quinceañera* and discuss how cloth is made.

Before transitioning to interest areas, point out the large looms created from a cardboard box that the children can use during choice time. Demonstrate how to use them. Use long strips of ribbon or rags to make it easier for children to weave.

Choice Time

As you interact with children in the interest areas, make time to

- Show children how they can work together while using the loom.

- Talk about the benefits of cooperation.

- Encourage children to explore the Internet to learn more about how cloth is made.

> **See Intentional Teaching Card LL26, "Searching the Web," for more information about supporting children's efforts to use the Internet as a resource.**

Read-Aloud

Read *Uncle Nacho's Hat.*

- **Before you read**, ask "What do you remember about this story?"

- **As you read**, define the words *appreciate* and *decent.*

- **After you read**, ask, "What do you think Uncle Nacho did with his old hat?" Invite the children to look at the last page of the book to see if they can find his hat.

English-language learners
When possible, read a book in a child's home language before reading it aloud in English.

Small Group

Option 1: Play Dough Weaving

- Review Intentional Teaching Card P02, "Play Dough Weaving."

- Encourage children to create strips of play dough and use them for weaving.

- Talk about the over-under technique and describe any patterns they create using different colors.

Option 2: Twisted Pretzels

- Review Intentional Teaching Card P03, "Twisted Pretzels." Follow the recipe with the children.

- Emphasize the over-under technique with the dough.

Mighty Minutes™

- Use Mighty Minutes 21, "Hully Gully, How Many?" Follow the guidance on the card.

Large-Group Roundup

- Recall the day's events.

- Invite children to share their experiences working at the looms.

Investigation 5

Where do we get our clothes?

	Day 1	Day 2
Interest Areas	**Toys and Games:** geoboards; geobands; shape cards	**Dramatic Play:** props for setting up a clothing store **Computer:** eBook version of *Button, Button, Who's Got the Button?*
Question of the Day	Where do you get your clothes? (Display choices, e.g., store, older sibling, present.)	How should we behave on our visit to the clothing store?
Large Group	**Music:** Rhythm Sticks **Discussion and Shared Writing:** Where and How Do People Get Their Clothes? **Materials:** rhythm sticks	**Song:** Mighty Minutes 23, "Hi-Ho, the Derry-Oh" **Discussion and Shared Writing:** Preparing for Site Visit or Visitor **Materials:** clipboards; pencils; Intentional Teaching Card SE01, "Site Visits"
Read-Aloud	*A Pocket for Corduroy*	*Button, Button, Who's Got the Button?*; a few small manipulatives for each child
Small Group	**Option 1: Rhyming Riddles** Intentional Teaching Card LL11, "Rhyming Riddles"; props **Option 2: Clothes Poem** Intentional Teaching Card LL10, "Rhyming Chart"; clothes poem that rhymes	**Option 1: Show Me Five** Intentional Teaching Card M16, "Show Me Five"; buttons **Option 2: Nursery Rhyme Count** Intentional Teaching Card M13, "Nursery Rhyme Count"; cotton balls; green construction paper
Mighty Minutes™	Mighty Minutes 07, "Hippity Hoppity, How Many?"	Mighty Minutes 24, "Dinky Doo"

Day 3	**Make Time For...**

Day 3

Dramatic Play: more clothing store props

Art: materials to make thank-you notes

What was your favorite part of the visit to the store?

Music: Rhythm Stick Patterns

Discussion and Shared Writing: What Other Items Do We Need for Our Store?

Materials: rhythm sticks; Mighty Minutes 26, "Echo Clapping"; *Mama and Papa Have a Store*

Something From Nothing

Option 1: Sly Salamanders

Intentional Teaching Card LL16, "Tongue Twisters"

Option 2: Same Sound Sort

Intentional Teaching Card LL12, "Same Sound Sort"; items that do and do not start with *S*; box or bag for storage

Mighty Minutes 18, "I'm Thinking Of..."

Make Time For...

Outdoor Experiences

Weaving Wall

- If you have access to a chain-link fence or a piece of lattice, you can use it to create a weaving wall. Tie long strips of fabric to the fence at a height the children can reach and invite them to move the fabric in and out of the open spaces.

Family Partnerships

- Ask families to send in pictures of family members in work clothes to use during Investigation 6, "What special clothes do people wear for work?"
- Invite a family member who wears a uniform to work and a family member who uses costumes for work or enjoyment to visit the classroom during Investigation 6, "What special clothes do people wear for work?"

Wow! Experiences

- Day 2: A site visit to a clothing store

Arrange to visit a clothing store during a time when the children can interview the manager or an employee.

Day 1   Investigation 5

Where do we get our clothes?

Vocabulary

English: *rhythm*

Spanish: *ritmo*

Large Group

Opening Routine

- Sing a welcome song and talk about who's here.

Music: Rhythm Sticks

- Give each child a set of rhythm sticks.

- Remind the children about the resting position they learned when they played with the drums.

- Wait until everyone is holding the sticks in the resting position before beginning.

- Explain, *"Rhythm* is the beat you hear in music." Tap your rhythm sticks to the tune of a familiar song. Encourage the children to join you.

Discussion and Shared Writing: Where and How Do People Get Their Clothes?

- Ask children to think about how people get their clothes. Review the question of the day.

- Record their additional ideas on a chart with the question. Responses might include buying them at the store, sewing

them, getting them from a thrift store, and getting hand-me-down clothes.

- Talk with children about creating a pretend clothing store.

- Have them begin to generate a list of items they will need for the store.

- Record their ideas.

- Tell children that they will be going to a real clothing store the following day to learn more.

English-language learners

To enable English-language learners who are not yet comfortable answering questions in English to participate, ask the class to respond in unison when appropriate. Only call on an English-language learner to respond if he or she raises a hand or otherwise indicates a willingness to answer.

Before transitioning to interest areas, talk about the geoboards and shape cards that are in the Toys and Games area.

Choice Time

As you interact with children in the interest areas, make time to

- Observe how children are using the geoboards. Pay attention to their ability to recreate the shapes on the cards.

Read-Aloud

Read *A Pocket for Corduroy.*

- **Before you read**, ask, "What is this book about? What happens in this story?"

- **As you read**, invite the children to retell the story using the pictures as cues.

- **After you read**, discuss how Corduroy got his clothes (his pocket) from Lisa. Ask the children if anyone they know has ever made clothes for them.

Small Group

Option 1: Rhyming Riddles

- Review Intentional Teaching Card LL11, "Rhyming Riddles." Follow the guidance on the card using clothing as the topic.

Option 2: Clothes Poem

- Find a short poem about clothes that rhymes.

- Review Intentional Teaching Card LL10, "Rhyming Chart."

- Read the poem to the children. Emphasize the idea that many poems have rhyming words.

- Reread the rhyming words and write them on a chart.

- Follow the guidance on the card to help children generate words that rhyme with *hat*.

- Continue with other words as long as it interests the children.

English-language learners
Accept approximations of sounds as children try to generate English words that rhyme with *hat*.

Mighty Minutes™

Use Mighty Minutes 07, "Hippity Hoppity, How Many?" Follow the guidance on the card.

Large-Group Roundup

- Recall the day's events.
- Invite children to share some of the rhyming words they discovered during small-group time.

Where do we get our clothes?

Vocabulary

English: *manager, salesperson, cashier*

Spanish: *administrador(a), vendedor(a), cajero(a)*

Large Group

Opening Routine

- Sing a welcome song and talk about who's here.

Song: "Hi-Ho, the Derry-Oh"

- Review Mighty Minutes 23, "Hi-Ho, the Derry-Oh."

Discussion and Shared Writing: Preparing for the Site Visit

- Ask the children what they would like to ask the manager or clerk. Record their questions.

- Tell them that they can use their clipboards to record anything interesting that they see at the store.

- Review the question of the day.

- Remind them about expectations for their behavior, e.g., stay together as a group and keep their hands to themselves unless a grown-up invites them to touch something. You should also remind them that everyone is responsible for holding his or her own observation clipboards and pencils. (See Intentional Teaching Card SE01, "Site Visits.")

> **Always prepare the person at the site you are visiting. Explain what the children will do and how this is different from typical site visits.**

Before transitioning to interest areas, talk about the clothing store props in the Dramatic Play area and how children can use them.

Choice Time

As you interact with children in the interest areas, make time to

- Observe their play in the pretend store.

- Encourage children to take on roles such as manager, salesperson, and cashier.

> **For more information on the levels of sociodramatic play, see *The Creative Curriculum for Preschool, Volume 2: Interest Areas.***

Read-Aloud

Read *Button, Button, Who's Got the Button?*

- **Before you read**, have each child find a partner. Distribute small manipulatives, e.g., cotton balls, unifix cubes, small blocks, to each pair of partners.

- **As you read**, invite the partners to make groups of manipulatives that equal the number of items on the page.

- **After you read**, review their groupings. Tell the children that the book and the manipulatives will be in the Toys and Games area for them to use during choice time. Also tell them that the eBook will be available to them on the computer in the Computer area.

Small Group

Option 1: Show Me Five

- Review Intentional Teaching Card M16, "Show Me Five." Follow the guidance on the card using buttons as the manipulative.

Option 2: Nursery Rhyme Count

- Review Intentional Teaching Card M13, "Nursery Rhyme Count." Follow the guidance on the card.

Mighty Minutes™

- Use Mighty Minutes 24, "Dinky Doo." Follow the guidance on the card.

Large-Group Roundup

- Recall the day's events.
- Invite children to share what they learned on the site visit. Chart their ideas.

Where do we get our clothes?

Vocabulary

English: *tattered, splotched, splattered*

Spanish: *harapiento, manchado, salpicado*

Large Group

Opening Routine

- Sing a welcome song and talk about who's here.

Music: Rhythm Stick Patterns

- Give each child a set of rhythm sticks.

- Remind children of the resting position.

- Review Mighty Minutes 26, "Echo Clapping." Follow the guidance on the card using the rhythm sticks.

Discussion and Shared Writing: What Other Items Do We Need for Our Store?

- Ask, "What did you see at the store yesterday that you think we should add to our store in the Dramatic Play area?"

- Record their ideas.

- Read *Mama and Papa Have a Store*. Comment on the types of items sold in the store. Ask, "Are there things we saw in this book that we should add to our list?" Record the new ideas.

- Review the ideas listed and ask, "How can we get these items? Is there anything we can make? Is there something in the classroom already that we could use for this?"

Before transitioning to interest areas, talk about the additional props in the Dramatic Play area and the materials to make thank-you notes in the Art area. Discuss how children may use them.

Choice Time

As you interact with children in the interest areas, make time to

- Record their dictation on the cards. Invite them to do as much writing as they can, including signing their own names.

- Offer ideas if they don't know what to write on the card. Invite them to draw something they saw in the store yesterday. Recall the question of the day to help them think of other ideas.

Read-Aloud

Read *Something From Nothing*.

- **Before you read**, ask the children what they remember about the story.

- **As you read**, invite them to name what the grandfather will make next. Define the words *tattered*, *splotched*, and *splattered*.

- **After you read**, go back through the book and ask the children to think of other things the grandfather could have made. "What else could he have made with the fabric from the tie?"

Small Group

Option 1: Sly Salamanders
- Review Intentional Teaching Card LL16, "Tongue Twisters." Follow the guidance on the card using the phrase, "Seventy-seven sly salamanders sledded in the snow."

Option 2: Same Sound Sort
- Review Intentional Teaching Card LL12, "Same Sound Sort." Follow the guidance on the card using items that **do** and **do not** start with *S*.

> Focusing on words that have the same beginning sound (alliteration) helps children make letter–sound connections.

Mighty Minutes™

- Use Mighty Minutes 18, "I'm Thinking Of...." Follow the guidance on the card.

- Use items that the children probably saw in the store they visited. Talk about shapes and lines as well as color, texture, and function as you describe the item. "I'm thinking of something that has a curved line on the top, like a hook, and a triangle on the bottom. It holds the clothes on the rack so they don't fall on the floor. It starts with the /h/ sound."

Large-Group Roundup

- Recall the day's events.
- Invite children to share their experiences playing in the store in the Dramatic Play area.

Investigation 6

What special clothes do people wear for work?

	Day 1	Day 2	Day 3
Interest Areas	**Blocks:** play people in uniforms or work clothes; digital camera **Computer:** eBook version of *Who Wears What?*	**Dramatic Play:** work clothes	**Music and Movement:** rhythm sticks
Question of the Day	Which of these does a firefighter wear at work?	Does anyone in your family wear a uniform to work?	Is there a fire station in your neighborhood? (chart with *yes, no, I don't know* options)
Large Group	**Song:** "What Is My Job?" **Discussion and Shared Writing:** Exploring Workers' Clothes **Materials:** common job clothing, e.g., a firefighter's hat (if allowed), a doctor's coat, a camouflage uniform; *Who Wears What?*; Mighty Minutes 11, "What Is My Job?"; digital camera	**Music:** Rhythm Stick Patterns **Discussion and Shared Writing:** What Do Your Family Members Wear to Work? **Materials:** rhythm sticks; Mighty Minutes 26, "Echo Clapping"; photos of family members in work clothes	**Song:** "The People in Your Neighborhood" **Discussion and Shared Writing:** Questions to Ask the Visitors **Materials:** book created during the previous day's small-group experience; Mighty Minutes 01, "The People in Your Neighborhood"
Read-Aloud	*Who Wears What?*	*Uncle Nacho's Hat*	*Little Red Riding Hood* Book Discussion Card 04 (first read-aloud)
Small Group	**Option 1: Jumping Beans** Intentional Teaching Card LL05, "Jumping Beans"; bean-shaped cards; coffee can **Option 2: Walk a Letter** Intentional Teaching Card LL17, "Walk a Letter"; masking tape; alphabet cards or chart	**Option 1: Family Photo Book** Intentional Teaching Card LL04, "Bookmaking"; photos of family members in work clothes; tape or glue; bookbinding supplies **Option 2: What Kinds of Clothes Do People Wear to Work?** Intentional Teaching Card LL04, "Bookmaking"; magazines; scissors; tape or glue; bookbinding supplies	**Option 1: More or Fewer** Intentional Teaching Card M59, "More or Fewer Towers"; interlocking cubes; more–fewer spinner; numeral–quantity card or die **Option 2: What's More?** Intentional Teaching Card M19, "Which Has More?"; ice cube trays or egg cartons; resealable sandwich bag; collection of objects that are similar in size, e.g., counters, coins, colored chips
Mighty Minutes™	Mighty Minutes 15, "Say It, Show It"	Mighty Minutes 10, "Words in Motion"	Mighty Minutes 25, "Freeze"

Day 4	Day 5	Make Time For…
Toys and Games: button and lacing boards	Dramatic Play: costumes	**Outdoor Experiences**

Physical Fun

- Intentional Teaching Card P14, "Moving Through the Forest" |
| Do you have an uppercase *D* or a lowercase *d* in your name? | Do you have a lowercase *e* in your name? | **Family Partnerships**

- Continue to ask families to send in photos of family members in work clothes to use in this week's investigation. Offer to take photos of family members during drop-off time if they arrive in their work clothes. |
| **Rhyme:** "Diddle, Diddle, Dumpling"

Discussion and Shared Writing: Class Visitor Wearing a Uniform

Materials: Mighty Minutes 27, "Diddle, Diddle, Dumpling"; digital camera | **Rhyme:** "Diddle, Diddle, Dumpling"

Discussion and Shared Writing: Class Visitor Wearing a Costume

Materials: Mighty Minutes 27, "Diddle, Diddle, Dumpling"; digital camera | - Share the date of the end-of-study celebration with families.

- Post a sign in a prominent area encouraging families to continue gathering items for the clothing drive.

- Invite families to access the eBooks, *Who Wears What?* and *Little Red Riding Hood*. |
| *Llama Llama Red Pajama*
Intentional Teaching Card SE05, "Character Feelings" | *Little Red Riding Hood*
Book Discussion Card 04 (second read-aloud) | **Wow! Experiences**

- Days 4 and 5: Have someone who wears a uniform or costumes for work, recreation, or both come to the classroom |
| **Option 1: Story Problems**

Intentional Teaching Card M22, "Story Problems"; manipulatives

Option 2: Problems at a Clothing Store

Intentional Teaching Card M22, "Story Problems"; collection of clothes | **Option 1: Story Problems**

Intentional Teaching Card M22, "Story Problems"; manipulatives

Option 2: Problems at a Clothing Store

Intentional Teaching Card M22, "Story Problems"; collection of clothes | If a family member is unavailable, ask the cook, janitor, school crossing guard, or other school employee to visit in uniform. Call a local theater company to invite someone to visit in costume if there are no theatrical family members. If you can, arrange for a site visit to go backstage and see the costumes. |
| Mighty Minutes 12, "Ticky Ricky" | Mighty Minutes 14, "Scat Singing" | |

Day 1 Investigation 6

What special clothes do people wear for work?

Vocabulary

English: *uniform*

Spanish: *uniforme*

Large Group

Opening Routine

- Sing a welcome song and talk about who's here.

Song: "What Is My Job?"

- Review Mighty Minutes 11, "What Is My Job?"

- Follow the guidance on the card using uniform clothing items.

- Invite the children to clap once for each word in the refrain, "What is my job? Can you guess?"

Discussion and Shared Writing: Exploring Workers' Clothes

- Introduce this investigation with a discussion. You might say, "People in certain jobs wear special clothes. Some wear uniforms. Think about firefighters. What clothes do they wear?"

- Continue with a few more examples, such as police officers, car mechanics, farmers, cooks, carpenters, athletes, dancers, or members of the military.

- Show the children some work clothes or pictures from the book, *Who Wears What?*

- Review the question of the day.

- Ask questions to help the children think about why certain jobs require certain uniforms, e.g., "Why do you think firefighters wear hard hats?"

English-language learners

If children seem puzzled by a particular question, use easier vocabulary and, if possible, a shorter, simpler sentence. For example, change "Why do you think firefighters wear hard hats at work?" to "Why do firefighters wear hats?" This technique, which benefits all children, is especially helpful for English-language learners.

Before transitioning to interest areas, talk about the play people in uniforms or work clothes in the Block area and explain how children can use them.

Choice Time

As you interact with children in the interest areas, make time to

- Observe how they use the play people in the Block area. Ask them about their constructions and what the people in uniform are doing.

- Photograph their constructions.

Read-Aloud

Read *Who Wears What?* (Read the first half of the book that describes what people wear for work.)

- **Before you read**, ask "What do you think this book is about?"

- **As you read**, pause and encourage the children to guess who wears the items of clothing described in the book.

- **After you read**, talk about what clothing items from the book are in the Dramatic Play area. Tell the children that the book will be available to them on the computer in the Computer area.

Small Group

Option 1: Jumping Beans

- Review Intentional Teaching Card LL05, "Jumping Beans." Follow the guidance on the card.

Option 2: Walk a Letter

- Review Intentional Teaching Card LL17, "Walk a Letter." Follow the guidance on the card.

Mighty Minutes™

- Use Mighty Minutes 15, "Say It, Show It." Follow the guidance on the card.

Large-Group Roundup

- Recall the day's events.

- Invite children who worked in the Block area to share what they did. Use the photographs you took as prompts.

Day 2   Investigation 6

What special clothes do people wear for work?

Vocabulary

English: *heartbreak*

Spanish: *partirse el corazón*

Large Group

Opening Routine

- Sing a welcome song and talk about who's here.

Music: Rhythm Stick Patterns

- Give each child a set of rhythm sticks.
- Remind children how to hold them in a resting position.
- Review Mighty Minutes 26, "Echo Clapping."
- Follow the guidance on the card with the children using the rhythm sticks.

Discussion and Shared Writing: What Do Your Family Members Wear to Work?

- Ask, "What kinds of clothes do your family members wear when they go to work?"
- Remind children about the question of the day.
- Invite children to share family photos that have been brought in.
- Record the words children use to describe the clothes.

Before transitioning to interest areas, point out the work clothes in the Dramatic Play area and talk about how children can use them.

Choice Time

As you interact with children in the interest areas, make time to

- Encourage them to explore the clothing collection for items that resemble the ones worn by family members in the pictures shared at large-group time.

Read-Aloud

Read *Uncle Nacho's Hat*.

- **Before you read**, cover the title and ask, "What is the title of this story?"

- **As you read**, encourage the children to retell the story by asking them to describe what is happening in the pictures and talk about what will happen next.

- **After you read**, turn back to the page where Uncle Nacho takes the hat to the country to leave it behind. Ask, "Uncle Nacho says he's leaving his hat here so his *heart won't break*. What do people mean when they say their heart breaks or they have a broken heart?"

English-language learners
Explain slang, idioms, and figures of speech that appear in children's books. Most young children are literal thinkers, so they may miss meaning or nuance in a story if they haven't heard common English expressions before or don't understand them.

Small Group

Option 1: Family Photo Book

- Review Intentional Teaching Card LL04, "Bookmaking." Follow the guidance on the card to create a book using the family photos that family members brought in.

Option 2: What Kinds of Clothes Do People Wear to Work?

- Review Intentional Teaching Card LL04, "Bookmaking."

- Have children look through magazines to find pictures of people dressed in work clothes and cut them out.

- Follow the guidance on the card to create the book.

Mighty Minutes™

- Use Mighty Minutes 10, "Words in Motion." Try the number variation on the back of the card.

Large-Group Roundup

- Recall the day's events.

- Share the book the children made during small-group time.

What special clothes do people wear for work?

Vocabulary

English: *neighborhood*

Spanish: *vecindario*

See Book Discussion Card 04, *Little Red Riding Hood* (*Caperucita roja*), for additional words.

Large Group

Opening Routine

- Sing a welcome song and talk about who's here.

Song: "The People in Your Neighborhood"

- Review the question of the day.

- Review Mighty Minutes 01, "The People in Your Neighborhood."

- Follow the guidance on the card.

- Add verses for the jobs depicted in the book the children created during small-group time the previous day.

Discussion and Shared Writing: Questions to Ask the Visitors

- Tell the children that visitors will be coming to the classroom to show and talk about their work clothes.

- Ask, "What questions do we want to ask our visitors during the next few days?

- Record their questions so that you can review them together before and after each visit.

Before transitioning to interest areas, talk about the rhythm sticks in the Music and Movement area and how children can use them.

Choice Time

As you interact with children in the interest areas, make time to

- Observe children using rhythm sticks.

- Listen for patterns in their playing.

- Encourage them to take turns creating a pattern and listening to and repeating other people's patterns.

Read-Aloud

Read *Little Red Riding Hood.*

- Use Book Discussion Card 04, "Little Red Riding Hood." Follow the guidance on the card for the first read-aloud.

Small Group

Option 1: More or Fewer

- Review Intentional Teaching Card 59, "More or Fewer Towers." Follow the guidance on the card.

Option 2: Which Has More?

- Review Intentional Teaching Card M19, "Which Has More?" Follow the guidance on the card.

Mighty Minutes™

- Use Mighty Minutes 25, "Freeze." Try the letter–sound variation on the back of the card.

Large-Group Roundup

- Recall the day's events.
- Remind children of the visitor who will be coming tomorrow.

Day 4 Investigation 6

What special clothes do people wear for work?

Vocabulary

English: *protect, patient*

Spanish: *proteger, paciente*

Large Group

Opening Routine

- Sing a welcome song and talk about who's here.

Rhyme: "Diddle, Diddle, Dumpling"

- Refer to Mighty Minutes 27, "Diddle, Diddle, Dumpling," and write the rhyme on a chart. Display the chart.

- Review Mighty Minutes 27, "Diddle, Diddle, Dumpling." Follow the guidance on the card.

- Point to the words on the chart as you read them. Casually call the children's attention to an uppercase *D* and a lowercase *d*.

- Invite the children to make up silly words for the rhyme, such as "middle, middle, mumpling."

- Invite children to come up to the chart and point to an uppercase *D* or a lowercase *d*.

- Review the question of the day.

> Substituting one sound (phoneme) for another is an advanced level of phonological awareness and a key predictor of future reading success.

Discussion and Shared Writing: Class Visitor Wearing a Uniform

- Introduce the visitor.

- Invite the visitor to explain his or her job and uniform.

- Invite the children to ask their questions, which you recorded yesterday. Record the responses.

- Explain that some of the clothes that people wear at work are designed to *protect* them, e.g., keep them from getting hurt or burned.

- Give an example of wearing a helmet while riding a tricycle.

- Take photos to document the visit and review later.

Before transitioning to interest areas, talk about the button and lacing boards in the Toys and Games area and talk about how children can use them.

Choice Time

As you interact with children in the interest areas, make time to

- Observe children's fine-motor coordination as they use the button and lacing boards.

- Describe their actions. "You are pulling the lace through the hole. Now you are making two loops."

> Some children in your classroom may need particular help developing fine motor strength and coordination. Buttoning and lacing give them opportunities to strengthen the muscles in their hands that they will use for writing.

Read-Aloud

Read *Llama Llama Red Pajama*.

- **Before you read**, ask, "What do you remember about this story?"

- **As you read**, describe the expressions on baby llama's face to call attention to his escalating feelings.

- **After you read**, turn to the page where mama says to be patient. Ask, "What does his Mama mean when she says, 'Please be *patient*?'" Further define the term if needed. Explain, "There are times when we need to be *patient* in our classroom, like when we wait in line at the water fountain." Ask, "When was a time you were *patient* in our classroom?"

> For more information about talking to children about feelings in books, see Intentional Teaching Card SE05, "Character Feelings."

Small Group

Option 1: Story Problems

- Review Intentional Teaching Card M22, "Story Problems." Follow the guidance on the card.

Option 2: Problems at a Clothing Store

- Review Intentional Teaching Card M22, "Story Problems."

- Follow the guidance on the card to create story problems about a clothing store. Use clothing from the collection as props, e.g., "I want to buy two green shirts and three blue shirts. How many shirts am I buying altogether?"

Mighty Minutes™

- Use Mighty Minutes 12, "Ticky Ricky." Follow the guidance on the card.

Large-Group Roundup

- Recall the day's events.

- Talk about the class visitor and write a group thank-you note. Invite the children to add drawings and to write their names on the note.

- Remind children that a visitor will be coming tomorrow.

What special clothes do people wear for work?

Vocabulary

See Book Discussion Card 04, *Little Red Riding Hood* (*Caperucita roja*), for words.

Large Group

Opening Routine

- Sing a welcome song and talk about who's here.

Rhyme: "Diddle, Diddle, Dumpling"

- Review Mighty Minutes 27, "Diddle, Diddle, Dumpling." Follow the guidance on the card.

- Display the Mighty Minutes 27, "Diddle, Diddle, Dumpling" chart from yesterday.

- Point to the words on the chart as you read them. Casually call the children's attention to a lowercase *e*.

- Invite the children to make up silly words for the rhyme, such as "biddle, biddle, bumpling."

- Invite the children to come up to the chart and point to a lowercase letter *e*.

- Review the question of the day.

Discussion and Shared Writing: Class Visitor Wearing a Costume

- Introduce the visitor.

- Invite the visitor to explain his or her job and the costume he or she wears.

- Invite the children to ask their questions. Record the responses.

- Help children to connect their own experiences with costumes, e.g., props in Dramatic Play area, Halloween costumes, or the costume the visitor wears to perform.

- Discuss what it means to pretend to be someone else. Ask the visitor about his or her experiences pretending.

- Take photos to document the visit and refer to later.

Before transitioning to interest areas, talk about the costumes available in the Dramatic Play area and how children can use them.

Choice Time

As you interact with children in the interest areas, make time to

- Describe what you see children doing with the costumes in the Dramatic Play area and ask questions about what they are doing.

> **By talking about what children are doing, you make them more aware that they are pretending.**

Read-Aloud

Read *Little Red Riding Hood.*

- Use Book Discussion Card 04, "Little Red Riding Hood." Follow the guidance for the second read-aloud.

Small Group

Option 1: Story Problems

- Review Intentional Teaching Card M22, "Story Problems." Follow the guidance on the card.

> **Repeating this small-group activity from the day before allows you to build on children's experiences and knowledge.**

Option 2: Problems at a Clothing Store

- Review Intentional Teaching Card M22, "Story Problems."

- Follow the guidance on the card to create story problems about a clothing store. Use clothing from the collection as props, e.g., "I want to buy two green shirts and three blue shirts. How many shirts am I buying altogether?"

Mighty Minutes™

- Use Mighty Minutes 14, "Scat Singing." Follow the guidance on the card.

Large-Group Roundup

- Recall the day's events.
- Discuss what the children learned from the visitor today and write a group thank-you note. Invite the children to add drawings and to write their names on the note.

Investigation 7

What other special clothes do people wear?

	Day 1	Day 2
Interest Areas	Art: butcher paper; paints; fabric scraps; glue; markers Computer: eBook version of *Little Red Riding Hood*	Art: butcher paper; paints; fabric scraps; glue; markers Computer: eBook version of *Who Wears What?*
Question of the Day	Is Little Red Riding Hood a real person or pretend character?	What do you put on first when you get dressed in the morning? Your socks, your underwear, or your shirt?
Large Group	**Game:** Rhythm Sticks Cooperation **Discussion and Shared Writing:** Clothing for Playing **Materials:** rhythm sticks; *Who Wears What?*	**Song:** "This Is the Way That We Get Dressed" **Discussion and Shared Writing:** Special Events **Materials:** Mighty Minutes 06, "This Is the Way"
Read-Aloud	*Little Red Riding Hood* Book Discussion Card 04 (third read-aloud)	*Who Wears What?*
Small Group	**Option 1: I'm Thinking of a Shape** Intentional Teaching Card M02, "I'm Thinking of a Shape"; geometric solids; empty containers shaped like geometric solids **Option 2: Straw Shapes** Intentional Teaching Card M42, "Straw Shapes"; geometric shape cards; drinking straws cut into different lengths; pipe cleaners	**Option 1: Tongue Twisters** Intentional Teaching Card LL16, "Tongue Twisters" **Option 2: Sorting C** Intentional Teaching Card LL12, "Same Sound Sort"; items that **do** and **do not** start with a hard *c* sound
Mighty Minutes™	Mighty Minutes 24, "Dinky Doo"	Mighty Minutes 15, "Say It, Show It"

Day 3	Make Time For...
Art: butcher paper; paints; fabric scraps; glue; markers **Dramatic Play:** photo album or family photos	## Outdoor Experiences **Shape Hunt** • Bring shape cards outside. • Invite children to select a shape card and then find objects outside that are the same shape as that on the card. • Take photos or let the children take pictures of what they find.
What special event has your family attended?	## Family Partnerships • Ask families to bring in photos of family events, e.g., a big brother's soccer game, a wedding, a holiday celebration, a beach trip. • Invite families to bring in items for the clothing drive.
Game: Leaping Sounds **Discussion and Shared Writing:** Special Family Events **Materials:** Mighty Minutes 17, "Leaping Sounds"; pictures of families at special events	
The Girl Who Wore Too Much	
Option 1: Letters, Letters, Letters Intentional Teaching Card LL07, "Letters, Letters, Letters;" alphabet stamps; ink pads; construction paper or magnetic letters and board. **Option 2: Buried Treasures** Intentional Teaching Card LL21, "Buried Treasures"; magnetic letters; large magnet; ruler or similar object; tape; sand table with sand	
Mighty Minutes 04, "Riddle Dee Dee"	

Investigation 7

What other special clothes do people wear?

Vocabulary

English: *straight*

Spanish: *recto*

See Book Discussion Card 04, *Little Red Riding Hood (Caperucita roja)*, for additional words.

Large Group

Opening routine

- Sing a welcome song and talk about who's here.

Game: Rhythm Sticks Cooperation

- Give each child two rhythm sticks.

- Explain that instead of making music with the rhythm sticks, they are going to make shapes.

- Point out that rhythm sticks have straight lines.

- Draw a shape that has only straight lines on chart paper. Count the number of straight lines on the shape.

- Ask the children to work with each other to create that shape using their rhythm sticks, e.g., if the shape is a rectangle, two children might put their pair of sticks together to form the shape or three children might use six sticks to make a rectangle.

- Describe the many ways that the children combined their sticks to make the shape. If there is no variety, ask, "Can you make that same shape using more [or fewer] sticks?"

- Continue using other shapes.

Discussion and Shared Writing: Clothing for Playing

- Explain that when people play sports, they sometimes wear special clothes.

- Show a few examples from the book, *Who Wears What?*

- Ask the children for other examples of special clothes that people might wear when they play.

- Record their responses.

Before transitioning to interest areas, talk about the materials in the Art area that the children can use to make a class mural. Invite them to represent something they have learned about clothes on the mural.

Choice Time	As you interact with children in the interest areas, make time to • Help children look back through charts from large-group times, photos taken throughout the study, children's artwork on the walls, and books they've made during small-group time to get ideas for the mural and reflect on their learning.	Making a mural together is an excellent way to promote cooperation and build a sense of community by working together. For more information about mural making, see Intentional Teaching Card SE26, "Making a Mural."
Read-Aloud	Read *Little Red Riding Hood*. • Use Book Discussion Card 04, "Little Red Riding Hood." Follow the guidance on the card for the third read-aloud.	• Review the question of the day. • Tell the children that the book will be available to them on the computer in the Computer area.
Small Group	**Option 1: I'm Thinking of a Shape** • Review Intentional Teaching Card M20, "I'm Thinking of a Shape." Follow the guidance on the card.	**Option 2: Straw Shapes** • Review Intentional Teaching Card M42, "Straw Shapes." Follow the guidance on the card.
Mighty Minutes™	• Use Mighty Minutes 24, "Dinky Doo." Follow the guidance on the card.	
Large-Group Roundup	• Recall the day's events. • Share the progress made on the class mural. Invite children who worked on it to share their contributions to the work.	• Talk about the clothing drive with the children. Remind them about their experience at the store and that clothing costs money. Explain that instead of throwing clothes away when they are too small for us or we don't need them anymore, we can donate them to other people who need them.

What other special clothes do people wear?

Vocabulary

English: *sequence*

Spanish: *secuencia*

Large Group

Opening Routine

- Sing a welcome song and talk about who's here.

Song: This Is the Way That We Get Dressed

- Review Mighty Minutes 06, "This Is the Way."

- Using the sequence of getting dressed, follow the guidance on the card.

- Explain, "We are going to sing a song about the *sequence* of getting dressed in the morning. A *sequence* is the order of what happens first, next, and last. We're going to start our song with the item of clothing that got the most votes in answer to our question of the day."

- Ask, "Which answer had the most votes this morning?"

- Continue with other verses, asking children what comes next in the sequence.

English-language learners

When asking the question of the day, show children the items you are naming. Then when leading the class in the song, point to each item to reinforce the vocabulary.

Discussion and Shared Writing: Special Events

- Recall a time that you attended a special event. Describe the event to the children and talk about what you and other people wore.

- Ask the children whether they can think of special events that they have attended where they had to wear special clothes.

- Invite children to share their stories. Record how they describe the clothing they wore.

Before transitioning to interest areas, talk about the materials in the Art area that children can use to make a class mural.

Choice Time

As you interact with children in the interest areas, make time to

- Continue to help children look back through charts from large-group times,

photos taken throughout the study, children's artwork on the walls, and the books they've made during small-group time to get ideas for the mural and reflect on their learning.

Read-Aloud

Read *Who Wears What?* This time, read the second part of the book that describes what clothes people wear for play and celebrations.

- **Before you read**, remind the children that you read the first part of the book, which describes the clothes people might wear to work. Say, "Now we're going to read about other special clothes that people sometimes wear."

- **As you read**, pause and invite the children to guess who wears the items of clothing you describe.

- **After you read**, ask, "Have you ever worn any of the clothes that we just read about in our book?" Invite the children to describe when and why they wore those clothes. Tell the children that the book will be available to them on the computer in the Computer area.

English-language learners
Breaking a long reading into two or more segments helps English-language learners as well as English-speaking children stay focused and comprehend the book.

Small Group

Option 1: Tongue Twisters
- Review Intentional Teaching Card LL16, "Tongue Twisters." Follow the guidance on the card using words that start with a hard *c* sound. Use the following tongue twister to start: "Cunning cats catch canaries in cages."

Option 2: Sorting C
- Review Intentional Teaching Card LL12, "Same Sound Sort." Follow the guidance on the card using items that **do** and **do not** begin with a hard *c* sound.

Mighty Minutes™

- Use Mighty Minutes 15, "Say It, Show It."

- Use shape cards to play the game. Invite children to say the name of the shape and show where else they can find that shape in the classroom.

Large-Group Roundup

- Recall the day's events.
- Share the progress made on the class mural. Invite children who worked on it to share their contributions to the work.

- Create an announcement to hang in the room, inviting families to an end-of-the-study celebration.

What other special clothes do people wear?

Vocabulary

English: *inspiration*

Spanish: *inspiración*

Large Group

Opening Routine

- Sing a welcome song and talk about who's here.

Game: Leaping Sounds

- Review Mighty Minutes 17, "Leaping Sounds." Follow the guidance on the card.

Discussion and Shared Writing: Special Family Events

- Invite the children to share pictures of their families at special events.

- Review the question of the day.

- Talk about the clothes that people are wearing and why they are wearing them, e.g., "Donovan's family reunion was at the beach, so everyone is wearing shorts and T-shirts; Jamile was the ring bearer in a fancy wedding, so he is wearing a tuxedo."

- As you talk about the pictures, put them in a photo album.

- Record some of the words children use to describe the clothing.

Before transitioning to interest areas, talk about the album of family photos in the Dramatic Play area and how children can use it as their *inspiration*—to give them ideas about pretend play. Remind children that they may continue to work on the mural in the Art area.

Choice Time

As you interact with children in the interest areas, make time to

- Invite children to use the family photos as inspiration for their play.

- Continue helping children as needed to represent their learning throughout the study on the class mural.

Read-Aloud

Read *The Girl Who Wore Too Much.*

- **Before you read**, ask, "Do you remember what this story is about?"

- **As you read**, talk about the special clothes the girl wants to wear for the dance.

- **After you read**, ask, "The girl in this story really wanted to look nice for the dance. Have you ever spent a lot of time thinking about what to wear to a special place because you wanted to look nice? Where were you going?"

Small Group

Option 1: Letters, Letters, Letters

- Review Intentional Teaching Card LL07, "Letters, Letters, Letters." Follow the guidance on the card.

Option 2: Buried Treasure

- Review Intentional Teaching Card LL21, "Buried Treasures." Follow the guidance on the card.

Mighty Minutes™

- Use Mighty Minutes 04, "Riddle Dee Dee." Follow the guidance on the card.

Large-Group Roundup

- Recall the day's events.

- Share the finished mural. Invite children who worked on it to share their contributions to the work.

Further Questions to Investigate

How can we extend the study further?

If children are still engaged in this study and want to find out more, you might investigate additional questions, such as these:

- Where do people in our community go to buy cloth or fabric?

- What do people have to know to work in a clothing or fabric store?

- What kind of clothes did our grandparents wear when they were children?

- Who decides what clothes should look like?

- What clothes do people wear in different parts of the world?

> Are there additional questions that will help you extend this study?

Our Investigation

Our Investigation

	Day 1	Day 2	Day 3
Interest Areas			
Question of the Day			
Large Group			
Read-Aloud			
Small Group			
Mighty Minutes™			

Day 4	Day 5	Make Time For...
		Outdoor Experiences
		Family Partnerships
		Wow! Experiences

Our Investigation

Vocabulary

English:

Spanish:

Large Group

Choice Time

Read-Aloud

Small Group

Mighty Minutes™

Large-Group
Roundup

Celebrating Learning

Closing the Study

When the study ends—when most of the children's questions have been answered—it is important to reflect and celebrate. Plan a special way to celebrate their learning and accomplishments. Allow children to assume as much responsibility as possible for planning the activities. Here are some suggestions:

- Set up stations for children to show visitors how they investigated clothes.

- Take a field trip to a large clothing store.

- Invite families and other classes to a fashion show.

- Make a big class book, photo album, or panel that documents the clothes study.

- Make tie-dyed T-shirts, bandanas, or socks for everyone in the class.

The following pages provide daily plans for two days of celebration. Add your own and the children's ideas for how to best celebrate all of their learning.

Celebrating Learning

	Day 1	Day 2	
Interest Areas	**Dramatic Play:** the clothing for the clothing drive; boxes **Computer:** eBook version of *The Quinceañera*	**Library:** all of the books the children made during the study	
Question of the Day	What would you like to show our guests tomorrow at the celebration about the clothes study?	What was your favorite part of the clothes study?	
Large Group	**Game:** Rhythm Sticks Cooperation **Discussion and Shared Writing:** Preparing for the Celebration **Materials:** rhythm sticks	**Song:** "Purple Pants" (and feature special clothes) **Discussion and Shared Writing:** Sharing Special Clothes **Materials:** Mighty Minutes 03, "Purple Pants"	
Read-Aloud	*The Quinceañera*	*Caps for Sale*	
Small Group	**Option 1: What's Missing?** Intentional Teaching Card LL18, "What's Missing?"; clothing collection; large piece of paper or cardboard **Option 2: Memory Game** Intentional Teaching Card LL08, "Memory Games"; memory game or lotto game	**Option 1: How Many Clothes?** Intentional Teaching Card M06, "Tallying"; clothing collection; clipboards **Option 2: Different Kinds of Clothes** Intentional Teaching Card M02, "Counting & Comparing"; clothing collection	
Mighty Minutes™	Mighty Minutes 21, "Hully Gully, How Many?"	Mighty Minutes 04, "Riddle Dee Dee"	

Outdoor Experiences

Physical Fun

- Intentional Teaching Card P29, "Stop & Go." Follow the guidance on the card.

Family Partnerships

- Include families in the celebration.

Celebrating Learning

Let's plan our celebration

Vocabulary

English: *celebration*

Spanish: *celebración*

Large Group

Opening Routine

- Sing a welcome song and talk about who's here.

Game: Rhythm Sticks Cooperation

- Give each child two rhythm sticks.

- Explain that instead of making music or shapes with the rhythm sticks, they are going to make letters.

- Point out that rhythm sticks are straight.

- Draw a letter that has only straight lines on chart paper. Count the number of straight lines in the letter.

- Ask the children to work with each other to create that shape using their rhythm sticks, e.g., if the letter is an *E*, two children might put their sticks together to form the letter, or three children might use five sticks to make it.

- Continue using other letters with straight lines.

Discussion and Shared Writing: Preparing for the Celebration

- Talk about the *celebration* tomorrow.

- Remind the children about the question of the day.

- Ask the children what they want to share with families and guests about the study.

- Make a list and help children gather the items and create a display.

Before transitioning to interest areas, talk about the clothing drive items in the Dramatic Play area and the boxes for sorting.

Choice Time

As you interact with children in the interest areas, make time to

- Ask, "Can you help me sort the clothing items into women's, men's, and children's clothes?" Label a box with the name of each category.

- Invite children to also sort the clothing by size and then fold the clothes and place them in the appropriate boxes.

Read-Aloud

Read *The Quinceañera.*

- **Before you read**, say, "We're having a celebration tomorrow. This book is about a different kind of celebration. What do they celebrate in this story?"

- **As you read**, ask, "How do you think the girl is feeling?"

- **After you read**, ask, "What special things do you do to celebrate birthdays in your family?" Tell the children that the eBook will be available to them on the computer in the Computer area.

Small Group

Option 1: What's Missing?

- Review Intentional Teaching Card LL18, "What's Missing?" Follow the guidance on the card.

Option 2: Memory Game

- Review Intentional Teaching Card LL08, "Memory Games." Follow the guidance on the card.

Mighty Minutes™

- Use Mighty Minutes 21, "Hully Gully, How Many?" Follow the guidance on the card.

Large-Group Roundup

- Recall the day's events.
- Remind children to wear some of their favorite clothes to school tomorrow.

Celebrating Learning

Let's celebrate

Vocabulary

English: *characteristic*

Spanish: *característica*

Large Group

Opening Routine

- Sing a welcome song and talk about who's here.

Song: "Purple Pants"

- Review Mighty Minutes 03, "Purple Pants."

- Follow the guidance on the card.

- Encourage the children to adapt the song to focus on a special *characteristic* of each child's clothing, e.g., "Jessica wore a lacy dress. She wore a lacy dress."

Discussion and Shared Writing: Sharing Special Clothes

- Invite children and families to show and talk about the special clothes they wore to the celebration.

- Review the question of the day.

- Record some of their descriptions.

Before transitioning to interest areas, talk about the class books in the Library area and invite children to read class books with their families in this area.

Choice Time

As you interact with children in the interest areas, make time to

- Invite children to show their families the work they did during the Clothes Study.

Read-Aloud

Read *Caps for Sale.*

- **Before you read**, ask, "What do you remember about this book? What problem does the peddler have in this story?"

- **As you read**, pause occasionally and invite the children to provide the words.

- **After you read**, wonder aloud, "I wonder what those monkeys are doing now. What do you think they are doing?"

Asking open-ended questions can encourage children to use their imaginations and think creatively.

Small Group

Option 1: How Many Clothes?

- Review Intentional Teaching Card M06, "Tallying."

- Follow the guidance on the card to have the children tally the clothing items for the clothing drive.

Option 2: Different Kinds of Clothes

- Review Intentional Teaching Card M02, "Counting & Comparing."

- Follow the guidance on the card to have children count the different kinds of clothing in the clothing drive.

Mighty Minutes™

- Use Mighty Minutes 04, "Riddle Dee Dee." Try the number variation on the back of the card.

Large-Group Roundup

- Recall the day's events.

- Invite children to share their favorite ideas from the study.

Reflecting on the Study

What were the most engaging parts of the study?

Are there other topics that might be worth investigating?

If I were to change any part of the study, it would be:

Other thoughts and ideas I have:

Resources

Background Information for Teachers

Consider the materials from which clothes are made. Natural materials are made from fibers of animal coats, silkworm cocoons, and plants. Common natural fibers are wool, cotton, linen, silk, and ramie. Leather is also natural, because it comes from an animal. However, it is made from an animal's skin or hide, not woven from animal hair. **Synthetic fibers** begin as liquid chemicals and are later woven or knit into fabric. Color is usually added to the liquid stage of synthetic fibers, so they are difficult to dye again once they have been made into fabrics. Some common synthetic fibers include polyester, nylon, acrylic, acetate, rayon, and spandex.

Think about the processes involved in manufacturing clothes. Whether clothes are made on a home sewing machine or in factories, the process is basically the same. First, a designer plans what the clothing will look like and creates a pattern. There is a pattern piece for each section of the clothing (sleeve, leg, collar, waistband, etc.). Then the pattern pieces are laid out on the fabric and the fabric is cut. All of the sections are then sewn together, and the garment is ironed or steamed.

Clothes serve a variety of purposes. Special types of clothing are designed and made for different climates and functions. Clothes vary depending on whether they are intended for formal or casual occasions, indoor or outdoor work, sports, or sleeping. Clothes for warm weather differ from those for cold weather.

Clothes vocabulary: *clothing, garments, attire, wardrobe, apparel, costume, outfit, suit, dress, neck, collar, cuff, sleeve, arm, leg, lapel, pocket, back, strap, waistband, belt, zipper, button, buttonhole, snap, hook-and-eye, seam, hem, tailor, seamstress*

Fabric vocabulary: *solid, print, patterned, striped, plaid, checked, polka dot, herringbone, denim, wool, velvet, corduroy, cloth, textile*

> **What do you want to research to help you understand this topic?**

Children's Books

In addition to the children's books specifically used in this *Teaching Guide*, you may with to supplement daily activities and interest areas with some of the listed children's books.

A New Coat for Anna (Harriet Ziefert)

All Kinds of Clothes (Jeri Cipriano)

All Sorts of Clothes (Hannah Reidy)

Argyle (Barbara Wallace)

Career Day (Anne Rockwell)

Charlie Needs a Cloak (Tomie de Paola)

Clean Clothes for Oliver (Andy Cooke)

Clothes (Dorling Kindersley Publishing)

Clothes (Karen Bryant-Mole)

Clothes (Robert Roper)

Clothes/La Ropa (Clare Beaton)

Clothes for Work, Play & Display (Jacqueline Morley)

Clothes From Many Lands (Mike Jackson)

Clothes in Colonial America (Mark Thomas)

Clothes of the Ancient World (Christine Hatt)

Clothes of the Early Modern World (Christine Hatt)

Clothes of the Medieval World (Vincent Douglas)

Clothes of the Modern World (Christine Hatt)

Community Helpers from A to Z (Bobbie Kalman)

Dan's Pants: The Adventures of Dan, the Fabric Man (Merle Good)

The Emperor's New Clothes (Hans Christian Andersen)

Farmer Brown Shears His Sheep: A Yarn About Wool (Teri Sloat)

Froggy Gets Dressed (Jonathan London)

I Like Old Clothes (Mary Ann Hoberman)

The Jacket I Wear in the Snow (Shirley Neitzel)

Jobs People Do (Christopher Maynard)

Joshua's Book of Clothes (Alona Frankel)

The Kettles Get New Clothes (Dayle Ann Dodds)

Kid's Clothes: From Start to Finish (Samuel Woods)

Knitting Nell (Julie Jersild Roth)

Let's Look at Clothes (Nicola Tuxworth)

Maisy's Favorite Clothes (Lucy Cousins)

Martha Moth Makes Socks (Cambria Evans)

Mary Wore Her Red Dress and Henry Wore His Green Sneakers (Merle Peek)

Ms. Moja Makes Beautiful Clothes (Jill Duvall)

My Clothes/Mi Ropa (Rebecca Emberly)

My First Book of How Things Are Made (George Jones)

My Very First Look At Clothes
(Christine Gunzi)

Red Berry Wool (Robyn Eversole)

Sam and the Tigers (Julius Lester)

Shoes, Shoes, Shoes; Hats, Hats, Hats
(Ann Morris)

*Snap, Button, Zip: Inventions to Keep
Your Clothes On* (Vicki Cobb)

Spotlight on Cotton (Lewis Miles)

Stinky Clothes (Joanna Emery)

The Surprise (Sylvia van Ommen)

Vejigante/Masquereder (Lulu Delacre)

Weaving the Rainbow (George Lyon)

Woolbur (Leslie Helakoski)

Warm Clothes (Gail Saunders-Smith)

What Can You Do With a Rebozo?
(Carmen Tafolla)

You'll Soon Grow Into Them, Titch
(Pat Hutchins)

Teacher Resources

The teacher resources
provide additional
information and ideas for
enhancing and extending
the study topic.

Clothing projects for children:
*Earth-Friendly Wearables: How to Make
Fabulous Clothes and Accessories from
Reusable Objects* (George Pfiffner)

Kids Weaving: Projects for Kids of All Ages
(Sarah Swett)

Science Experiments with Color
(Sally Nankivell-Aston)

*Songs from the Loom: A Navajo Girl
Learns to Weave* (Monty Roessel)

*Warm As Wool, Cool As Cotton: The Story
of Natural Fibers and Fabrics and How to
Work With Them* (Carter Houck)

Weaving Without a Loom
(Veronica Burningham)

You Can Weave: Projects for Young Weavers
(Monaghan & Joyner)

Weekly Planning Form

Week of: _____   Teacher: _____   Study: _____

	Monday	Tuesday	Wednesday	Thursday	Friday
Interest Areas					
Large Group					
Read-Aloud					
Small Group					

Outdoor Experiences:

Family Partnerships:

Wow! Experiences:

Weekly Planning Form, continued

"To-Do" List:

Reflecting on the week:

Individual Child Planning